Black Sparrow

Broxin Delano

BALBOA.
PRESS

A DIVISION OF HAY HOUSE

Balboa Press books may be ordered through booksellers or by contacting:

Balboa Press
A Division of Hay House
1663 Liberty Drive
Bloomington, IN 47403
www.balboapress.com
1-(877) 407-4847

Because of the dynamic nature of the Internet, any web addresses
or links contained in this book may have changed since publication
and may no longer be valid. The views expressed in this work are
solely those of the author and do not necessarily reflect the views of
the publisher, and the publisher hereby disclaims any responsibility
for them. Names of characters and locations have been changed.

The author of this book does not dispense medical advice or prescribe the use
of any technique as a form of treatment for physical, emotional, or medical
problems without the advice of a physician, either directly or indirectly. The
intent of the author is only to offer information of a general nature to help
you in your quest for emotional and spiritual well-being. In the event you use
any of the information in this book for yourself, which is your constitutional
right, the author and the publisher assume no responsibility for your actions.

ISBN: 978-1-4525-3232-5 (sc)
ISBN: 978-1-4525-3233-2 (e)

Printed in the United States of America
Balboa Press rev. date: 2/23/2011

Trying to convince someone to believe in God is about as pointless as praying to be straight, another race, or wealthy. Thank God that I believe in God. Depending on how I view my life, it could be fortunate or unfortunate that I am not straight, Caucasian, or wealthy. Unfortunately, I once obsessively prayed to be straight, denied my racial value, and fantasized about being filthy rich. Fortunately, I am just me; black, gay, financially comfortable, and remarkably proud of the individual that I have become.

I once told *Terminus* magazine in an interview, "I am who I imagined myself being as a child." This is true, but never did I imagine some of the roads I would travel to get here. In the fabric of my heart, I truly believe that everyone has a predetermined path in life. This is great and wonderful news considering that it is human nature to feel that you have a purpose and that your actions are validated through success and accomplishment.

I began to keep a journal when I discovered that I wanted to find out why I did some of the things that I did and moreover why I entertained some of my most self-destructive and emotionally excruciating thoughts. What motivates me and what makes me tick? What is the gasoline that fuels the behavior of my core being? I doubt that I will ever truly know or quite understand, but I feel that God is pleased that I care enough about His beautiful creation to even ponder these things. I resolve confirmation in knowing there are things I will never find the answers to as long as I am on earth. To possess such affirmations would be divinely cruel, provide an unfair advantage, and prove to be dramatically satisfying. Subsequently, I feel this work should be dedicated to anyone who cares to read it and who understands what at times I could not.

St. Ignatius

My earliest memory of Christ is having a vision of Him flying across the sky of my preschool playground. It was a glorious sight! I specifically remember how angelic Jesus appeared, daunting immense wings and a billowing trail of white blazing smoke. In divine astonishment, I pointed my four-year-old finger shouting, "Look! It's Jesus!" My slightly less amused peers quickly shattered my perceived vision by identifying this avail object as an airplane and dismissing my foolish accusations. But I was neither deterred nor jaded. I simply continued to gaze up at this figure, watching our savior smiling down upon me. Smiling back, I waved and knew from that moment that Jesus indeed loved me.

St. Ignatius is an Episcopal church in downtown Virginia Beach, Virginia. There is a modest congregation that has dwindled over the years, but conclusively, it is a stable church community. A majority of the youth from my generation at St. Ignatius have turned out to be decent American citizens. Of course, there were the occasional drug or violence related incarcerations, single parenthood, and various other shameful, anti-social behaviors, but to counter balance the negative gossip, the "gossip hounds" would always mention the college graduates, individuals who married well, and various prideful, social behaviors that share no relationship with Christ.

Being dragged out of bed and forced to attend Sunday Service is never the best way to be presented with Christianity. Nevertheless, my brother, Paul, and I would go, resenting my mother and loathing every minute of it. As a child, sitting on the cushioned pew in the beautiful sanctuary of St. Ignatius Episcopalian and Apostolic Church was similar to playing a game of Duck Duck Goose. We were scattered throughout the congregation with our respective families waiting for a voice to crack in the choir, or someone to walk in looking terrible, or a letter to get passed with some adolescent joke on it, before beginning to jump and cut up.

Getting through the service could be a challenge, but my favorite part was at the end when Father Thymes would proclaim, "Let us go forth into the world rejoicing in the power of the spirit!" And the choir would close in soprano harmonies, "Thanks.....be.... to God....... Amen!" Imagine how magnificent the tympani drums would have sounded at this time, had St. Ignatius owned any.

When diagramming the story line of a literary work, there is typically an exposition, followed by rising action, leading to the climax, which then falls into a resolution. Church services are structured this same way. My least favorite memory of the service at St. Ignatius was the Exposition, or the cued greeting and offering of peace. Correct me if I am mistaken, but should you *not* have greeted everyone you cared to shake hands with before the service? Is it not extremely disturbing to be forced beyond one's comfort zone to smile in the face of the parents and friends of someone you would later gossip, fight, smoke a joint, or have sex with?

The rising action, the lessons, could prove to be either brain numbing or eternally and internally stimulating and gratifying. The sermons often seemed like peripheral noise and were seldom well received. I was probably wrong to enter the church expecting to hear a life-changing message. Later, I would discover that will power is the only catalyst for personal change. But, expecting a child to know this is preposterous. However, expecting a child to receive a spiritual message from an unbiased perspective is *completely* fathomable? The Climax is of course the communion, the repentance of the previous week's sins and the promise that, in Christ, we are born again. All of this then falls into the offering. In other words, "How much do you owe the church for this soul satisfying experience and peace of mind?" And the resolution: Unmistakably to go forth into the world rejoicing in the power of the spirit!

Honestly, I am grateful that my mother did drag my brother and me out of bed and into church. The rising action that was stimulating enough to pay attention to planted itself deep into the sponges of my mind. This would later prove to be important in influencing and molding me into the individual that I am today. As for the messages that were not well received; as an adult, I will and must take responsibility for this. Perhaps if I had been more attentive to Father Thymes and the Choir and less interested in playing Duck Duck Goose, I would have engaged and absorbed the temporary and external forgotten and unknown rising action.

My Brother Paul

Where do I begin with my brother Paul? His is probably one of the most devastating and tragic stories I have heard. As an infant, he was neglected and sodomized by a family member, my Grandmother's mentally ill sister: My great aunt, Ophelia. She was unfit to look after any child, but the family referral resumes leave out this information. So my young and naïve mother entrusted the life and care of her oldest son in the hands of her husband's mother's crazy sister. My mom dropped Paul off in the morning on her way to work and picked him up in the afternoon. By this time, Aunt Ophelia's daughter, very aware of her mother's mental illness, sexual promiscuity and coexisting drug addiction, would have cleaned up the evidence at the scene of the crime. She would get there in time to change Paul's feces and urine saturated diaper, feed him enough to stop the crying, and locate her mother who was down the street assumingly exchanging sexual favors for a fix. Only God knows how many days, weeks, or months this sadistic ritual continued.

To hear my mother tell Paul's story, it was a mother's intuition and divine intervention that steered her white 1977

Mercedes 280 towards Ophelia's depraved residence early from work one afternoon. An abandoned house met her with the front door swung wide open. She could hear the painful cries of her child from the street when she turned off the ignition of the car. Paul lay, kicking and screaming, in a pile of his own bodily expulsions with a halo of salt water around his head. Inherently feeling that there was something frighteningly wrong with this scene, my mother began to investigate. It was then that she discovered every bag of diapers, every jar of baby food, every toy, blanket, rattle, and pacifier untouched (with the exception of the one's used moments before her arrival). My mother does not remember removing him from his playpen and leaving Ophelia's den of iniquity because she was boiling over with the rage of a mother who has ever lost the *Battle by the Breadfruit Tree.*

The effects of this neglect lay dormant until the age of two and a half, when Paul began showing signs atypical of a healthy baby boy: He loss his appetite, began showing signs of skittishness, and was suffering from rectal bleeding. My self-blaming mother viewed most of these signs as rejection, and then she got the phone call that would change everything. It was Ophelia on the telephone, appropriately nicked named *Pedophilia* by family members unfortunate enough to be privy to what she did to Paul. This disturbed and demented, drug addicted prostitute proudly boasted about the objects that she impaled into my brother because he was crying too much. I never heard the conversation, but knowing my red blooded, Haitian dissented mother, it probably included some desperate and emotional death threats upon Aunt Pedophilia. But what could she do, the woman she wanted to murder being the aunt of the man she loved? She did what any loving mother and Christian would do; she turned the other cheek.

I was born a year and seven days after Paul. I remember being very close to Paul until he developed posttraumatic emotional and medical repercussions. Paul developed intestinal polyps and a severe and violent emotional disability. Subsequently, Paul was expelled from our elementary school for pushing a shelf of library books over on another student and showing up with a concealed kitchen knife. Because of the dangerous emotional behaviors and exceedingly worse medical complications, Paul was hospitalized for surgeries to correct the intestinal damage and spent his recovery time in a correctional facility that helped adolescents dealing with emotional trauma. He was absent for a great deal of my elementary and fundamental school development. My mother, father, and I would visit Foster Colonial on the weekends hoping that Paul had made progress in his emotional recovery. I did not miss the attention that my parents gave Paul and not me. In fact, I enjoyed having the freedom to do whatever I wanted to and have them barely notice. I wore my mother's high heels, sucked my fingers, kissed and pinched boys at school, and truly embraced my feminine side at a rate that was too bazaar yet enjoyable to articulate. Maybe my parents believed these behaviors were normal for a child who had not been molested or left without a mother from an infantile age for eight hours during the day.

Paul did get better, although he has not fully recovered. He remains unhuggable and extremely introverted, but this experience has given him a faith in God that is stronger than any chain-linked anchor securing the largest of aircraft carriers. He is one of the purest and most honorable Christian men I have ever had the pleasure of coming together in fellowship with. He actually practices Christianity beyond the resolution of service and into the weeks, days, hours, and minutes of his life. Not that this determines ones' relationship with God, but to the best of my knowledge, Paul is a virgin. I would not be surprised to find that he remains a virgin for the rest of his life. Maybe he is saving himself for marriage because it is deemed as God's way? Maybe he has intimacy issues that deem him sexually undesirable and completely incapable of completing the act. I cannot be certain, but whatever his pain, he has delivered it into the hands of the Lord and been born again.

My Crazy Aunt Madison

There are very few people who have impacted my life in a massive enough way to influence my personality. I debated whether or not to mention my Aunt Madison, adding this Chapter upon realizing that she was imperative to my story not only because I love her dearly, but also because we are such similar creatures. We are kindred spirits that supply the energy to the dials that rotate around our hearts, and our hearts are filled with loving and astronomical humor. Aunt is not the most brilliant person on earth. In fact, her flaws are appealing to me. It is wonderful getting lost in someone's flaws because upon understanding why these fallacies exist, it becomes apparent that they are really not flaws at all. Pondering Aunt's flaws forces me to question why I do not hold myself to this realization. Why is it easier to embrace another's flaws but not my own? A majority of my flaws are not tragic but more so just a trait that characterizes me as an individual. I believe that God plots all steps prior to conception. Our characteristics were stamped on us by His almighty hand before we were even a thought. This does not guarantee that our flaws will be easy to embrace, in fact, I frequently agonize over what I feel may be a flaw. I am who I am for a reason, God says so. I cannot understand my Aunt's flaws, but I love her because *and* in spite of them—She is stubborn, impulsive, inappropriate, crazy and unfiltered, and one of my favorite people on earth. Aunt flagrantly passes gas, chain smokes, exclusively shops at thrift stores (and concocts fabulous ensembles), makes whimsical life changing decisions, and possess a raw sense of humor that I find captivatingly mesmerizing. Being my mother's youngest sister, Aunt is one of the few people who knows how to push my mother's buttons, and this is sheer entertainment. Aunt finds a way to get my mother to completely embarrass herself without even realizing she has been made the brunt of her own humiliation, and then she will sit back and cackle, affording all who have witnessed my mother's demise the pleasure of enjoying a sibling rivalry that has carried on into womanhood. Of course Mom interprets Aunt's life as a catastrophic and dilatory disaster, however, I envisage Aunt's journey as gregariously fantastic!

I have often considered how things might have been different if Aunt gave birth to me? At times I have thought, with a slight level of embarrassment, "What if Aunt *was* my mother?" Aunt is big, black, and beautiful with something disturbingly tragic in her eyes. When I consider my Aunt's passion for life and blithe spirit, my personal focus on hypothetical differences in my life seem shallow and wasted, for she is a reminder to me that happiness is one of the resources we have the ability to create naturally. It is true that we are born and will die alone, but only Aunt seems to recognize that we live together, and she makes it an enjoyable and laughter filled ride. As far as Aunt's self-destructive indulgences, she may smoke KOOL filter kings to satisfy some need for which she does not have an outlet, her over the top sense of humor may be the expulsion of internalized grief, her relentless behavior could be the manifestation of her social normalcy inadequacies, and her impulsive and incomprehensible decisions could be her way of proving that God truly does care for her and will provide a means of survival despite the circumstances. It may be gratifying to not get so enraptured in life's painful ride. Quit your job and don't have retirement…so what? Bought a car and cannot afford it; broke is a state of mind… Who cares? And the hell with Ollie's father sleeping in a separate room; he is less than adequate in fulfilling my needs anyway. Aunt does not disguise her true feelings; she often transforms the most tragic events of her life into the substance of her most vulgar jokes. Maybe Aunt's vice is humor, but I see beyond the outrageous absurdity to a woman who so desperately wants to love and be loved by the Lord. I see a wonderful mother and the planet's most thoughtful Aunt. I may not be capable of adopting this vice and carefree perspective, but I admire her nonetheless and have found that in times of crisis, laughter can be an ultimate release.

Aunt learned how to play the piano by ear at a very young age, and through this blessing she and I have been able to come together and create beautiful music. These sessions mean everything to me because I feel we are both able to connect and channel a purity that we struggle to understand. Music has given us that venue to express our love for God together. While on earth, these opportunities are precious because our love for music has provided strength. Since I began playing the Clarinet at twelve years old, Aunt and I have been having impromptu "jam" sessions. As I have grown, these sessions have become more of a piano accompanied gospel hour that brings the entire family together to sing praise to the Lord. Presently, a visit home is not complete without my crazy Aunt Madison on the piano and me by her side.

Abuse and Empowerment

I was ten years old when I decided to write my father out of my life. I liquidated every ounce of respect a boy could have for his dad. My father was no addict, but definitely had a problem with drinking. He was a loathable bully and an intolerable drunk, until he lost the respect and love of his youngest son.

Doing arithmetic is not enjoyable for any fifth grader. Some might be good at it, but receiving enjoyment from mathematics is maturation-wise impossible. My teacher, Mrs. McEatren, had given some tedious assignment that required knowing the rules of that day's lesson in order to complete it. My father, who was *incorrectly* correcting my work over my shoulder, which I despise, had been chalkboard-scratch irritating the entire evening. He was insisting on changing the answers that I had to answers he felt were more appropriate. Not only were they wrong, but he also had the audacity to alter my work having not been present for the necessary lesson! So, I snatched the pencil from him and nudged him away with my elbow. He then beat me within an inch of my life. To this day, I have not been able to completely forgiven him. My mother tried to stop him, but he raised his hand to her and she backed down. He beat me from the dining room, into the foyer, down the hall, into the kitchen, and back into the dining room. I could see the room spinning as if I were having a seizure, and then it stopped. My father got on his knees and strangled me face-to-face until I felt all of the blood vessels in my eyes pop and my brain heat and swell starving for oxygen. I honestly thought I was going to die, and then he released me. It was at that instant that I realized that he did not love me. No one could ever do something like that to someone they loved. So, I convinced myself that I no longer loved my father, and wrote him out of my life at ten years old. Without a choice, I continued on living under his and my mother's roof, refraining from any social interaction with my father what so ever. Three years went by and I refused to utter a single word to the man. By not acknowledging his existence, I hoped to have sent a transparent and painful message to him. Everyday, I would pour salt on an open wound, making sure that he knew that he was responsible for the dissention in the household and for culminating another atrocity to an already utterly dysfunctional family.

Over time, I began to notice how my father would (always with physical intimidation) impose punishment on Paul, even when I was entirely and obviously (to any outside, neutral, or unbiased party) in the wrong. My father never laid another hand on me. This pleased me, so I began to call him Dad again. Occasionally I asked him for money or told him I would need a ride home from some after-school extracurricular engagement, but I never invited him into my life or cared to disclose any significant fragment of who I was to him. My Dad began trying to take interest in my interests. It was the least he could do after forcing me to play football, basketball, and baseball, all of which I attribute to being the most significant factors to my astronomically low self-esteem and even worse perception of worth. I was horrific at sports, and being forced to clumsily run drills, miss catches, fall on my face, under throw balls, run like a girl, and countless ghastly emasculating embarrassments in front of a squad of post- adolescence, pre-testosterone and at the time hormonal boys, heckling me with taunting words like, "You suck faggot," or, "What position do you play? Left bench," did not give my father any redemption points in my book of hostility held grudges. So, when he tried to take an interest in my true interest, the manifested hate kept me from giving a damn what he thought about my heart's passions, and still to this day, I could not care less.

Ironically, because of this experience I have endured a beautiful, self-fulfilling, and everlasting epiphany. Metaphorically, I have come to be who I am in layers. I created so many layers at such an early age that I lost who Broxin truly was. For example, trying to be more masculine lead me to feel a significant amount of unnecessary pain when I was called faggot. Had I just stayed true to myself, the term faggot would not have affected me in the slightest, and I would have told those people to just go to hell. Furthermore, by refusing to let someone who I felt did not love me hurt me, I became this person who subconsciously did not care if I hurt those who loved me the most. In doing this, the only people I was pleasing were those who did not give a damn about me. I needed to learn to forgive. Forgiveness has completely freed me from this painful situation with my father and all horrible experiences associated. I have gained insurmountable internal knowledge because of how this traumatic childhood event has affected me, but I have also learned how to give my pain up to the Lord. The reason why I carried this pain for so long is because it empowered me, but layer-by-layer, I have learned that I do not need to be in power. God is my strength, through Him comes all true and pure power. Everything else is just baggage. If I were more like God, then not only would I be able to forgive my dad, but I would also forget.

My mother and father were very well aware of what I was, all parents know, whether they choose to accept it or not. Hell, it was my mother's fault. I only say this because of countless episodes of her braiding my hair, me braiding hers, and her witnessing me twirling in her heels, panty hose, and chiffon while continuing to coddle and cherish me. In any case, my poor father was doomed to never get any respect from me because while trying to fight the reality that his son was effeminate, he forced me to participate in football, baseball, and basketball... and I loathed every minute of it and blamed and hated him for it. So it was no surprise to me that when I went to my parents with things that I enjoyed doing (music, dance, literature, and the creative arts) I was shot down at every angle.

When I was in fifth grade, I won a literary contest; The Media Festival. The winner of this writing competition went downtown and worked with a staff of people developing their story into a cartoon. This was by no means a Disney production, but to a ten-year-old, having audio and visual feedback for their work is a pretty big deal. My story was entitled *The Little Prince*, and was a massive allusion to the story of Moses. The main character was a young boy whose mother was too poor to raise him when he was an infant, so she reluctantly tucked him into a wicker basket and placed him in the upstream currents of a neighboring river headed towards an undetermined destination. The basket found itself in the kingdom of a ruler who was unwedded and without children. The king's heart was grief stricken with loneliness and a deep desire for a son, so he praised his servants for bringing him the child and raised it as his own. In his son's adolescent years, the king began to feel as if his little prince needed a mother, so the kingdom-wide search for a queen-bride began. The poetic justice occurs at the end of the story when the plot reveals that what the little prince did not know was that the king's new wife was his long lost mother… and they all lived happily ever after. I tried to win this contest for years writing stories that I thought were fantastical. But prior to writing *The Little Prince*, I had an overwhelmingly calm feeling. I knew it was my last opportunity to win this state wide elementary school contest. So, I wrote from my heart. I have seldom experienced the emotions of pure shock and joy simultaneously in my life, which is why I can remember vividly hearing my name called as The Media Festival winner over the intercom at school. I could not believe it! I had actually won something that was not sports related! But I did not have anyone to share my joy with; on the evening that I was to receive my award and present my production to the audience, neither of my parents were in the crowd. Fortunately for me, I lived close enough to my elementary school to ride my bike to the ceremony because being there alone was more rewarding than not being there at all. Unfortunately for me, it was this evening that I realized that in life I was going to do innumerable things on my own, and the only person I could depend upon was myself.

Alternatives to Gay

Middle school posed many obstacles for me. During puberty, the boys at my school seemed to be enchanted by the girls. Who was kissing whom and what base someone got to seemed to be all the rage. This was the time to have a girlfriend for a few months and then break up with her for something as minuscule as a clique change.

In sixth grade I was first propositioned by a chunky girl named Tijuana Downs. She called me on the telephone one evening and asked me if I would like to be her boyfriend. This intrigued me, so I asked her, "Why?" Tijuana told me that the relationship, if forged, would be doing us both a favor. This intrigued me as well, so I asked her, "How?" Tijuana explained that because of her weight she was all but desirable, and due to everyone's accusations that I was a fag, I needed a beard. Of course, her eleven-year-old vocabulary did not express the scenario in this manner, but revisiting this conversation, it was clear what she was trying to say. This news was earth shattering; I thought I was doing a remarkable job of perpetrating a heterosexual fraud. I had no choice but to accept! The thought of being called a fag was absolute torture. Bearing it would have been much more tolerable with an overweight girlfriend on my arm.

I remember praying to be delivered from being a faggot. I hoped that being a fag was some sort of phase that I would out grow. I speculated whether or not being a fag automatically meant I was going to be gay, and thus go to hell. I wasted so much energy and time cursing myself and trying to be what I thought everyone else wanted me to be that I lost track of who I was. And by becoming misguided and trying to be someone else, 'Broxin-the-packaged-good' began to become a marketable product. Because I was expelling maximum efforts to be as masculine as possible, being called a faggot would hurt even more.

My relationship with Tijuana lasted approximately two weeks. We kissed once, and it was horrifically disturbing. It was like two frogs trying to clean fly remains off the roof of each other's mouths. This was the last time I would have a girlfriend in middle school.

I began to truly discover my sexual being in seventh grade. My hormones were like a racquet ball trapped in its glass chamber, struggling desperately to bounce to freedom. As many twelve-year-old boys do, I became familiar with my urges and desires and the types of people I wanted to be around. This posed a debilitating problem, as all the other twelve-year-olds were having urges for the opposite sex. So I did what I believe many young, gay males and females do, I became an actor. An actor in my own life, playing a role that was a manifested emulation of what I hypothesized a heterosexual twelve-year-old boy was to be. I was miserable. The curtains would never go down, the credits refused to roll; even in what was supposed to be the comfort of my own home.

My life began to develop into a multi-dimensional catastrophe. Internally, I was juggling a young boy who enjoyed music, writing, classic movies, and theater, while being forced to play football, basketball, and baseball. I excelled at swimming and band and began to forge strong friendships with people I felt most comfortable around. But every other experience was utterly humiliating to the degree of esteem wrecking discomfort. At this juncture, my relationship with Paul grew more and more distant. He was beyond his emotional and behavioral outburst and had developed his own self-destructive and reduplicative idiosyncrasies to heal his torrential and painful memories. So I began to search for family outside the confines of blood and home. I truly cannot remember much about myself from seventh grade, and I believe that is because I have blocked it all out. Perhaps with a weird psychological analogy, I can explain that my seventh grade year in middle school is my 'middle-child' phase of development; ignored, insignificant, and desperately needing to be acknowledged and understood to engender my healthy development.

Eighth grade was a transitional year for me. I feel most of it was an Oscar winning performance. I had become accustomed to being on stage and had developed a significant fan base (mostly female), but I was untrue nonetheless and still silently praying that one-day I would marry, have kids, a white picket fence, and be *normal*. In retrospect, life has taught me to ask the question, *what is so great about white picket fences anyway?*

Towards the end of the school year, as everyone emotionally prepared to enter high school, I became nervous that my act was losing its luster. I mean, I was a thirteen-year-old black male who played the clarinet and hung out with a bunch of girls. And I am really not that talented of an actor. It was time for me to change the routine a little bit. I was too soft to be a thug and the black guys in the pre-thug program did not seem to be too enthused by the fact that I was in band and on the honor roll. I felt like an outcast from my black peers, so I did the only thing that made sense to me, I began to hang out with my Caucasian peers. I wore bajas and Doc Martens and listened to Toad the Wet Sprocket. I felt new, liberated, and most of all, accepted. There was something about the spectacle of being black and wearing outrageous clothing and hairstyles that afforded me comfort in my skin. Somewhere in the confusion of my mind, I felt it was less of an insult to be called an oreo than a faggot. And with my newly adopted mentality and image, on to high school I went.

Rebel With a Cause

I do not remember the first day of high school. I do remember what I wore though. I also remember waiting for the bus that day, getting to school, and recognizing that I was a single number in a sea of insignificance. But everything else was a memory that at the time, I knew I was going to replace with the first experience that took place in a different setting. I was miserable at my high school and hated every moment of every day. My mother sensed my discomfort and arranged a hardship transfer to the high school of my choice, Kikotan High School—GO FIGHT WIN! Now Kikotan was not just any high school. Kikotan was notorious, and I would not have had it any other way. Kikotan was the first high school in the history of public schools to have two people of the same sex attend prom together. It earned our blazing Alma Mater, Virginia Beach's widely recognized heckle of 'Kick a Fag' High School. The finalizing and documenting newspaper article, featuring photographs of the two guys who built up enough courage to ask each other, remained on display in the school library for all to behold. And if that was not enough to make my school attractively enchanting, on the newly created World Wide Web in 1996, we were ranked as the sixth high school in the country where LSD was most readily available. And to confirm this liberal creed, I remember buying such product for $5.00, on occasional early release days, as tripping acid in school was a 'rave/skater crew' rite of passage. The drug was meticulously packaged in a stick of chewing gum, neatly positioned underneath the wrapping. I would disclose personal documentation of incidents that took place in the halls of KHS if it weren't for sheer embarrassment and strength of nark control.

One of the most memorable experiences from my sophomore year turned out to be an insignificant tryst involving a senior, Tonyagene Tess. She was beautiful, popular, thrifty, and sexy, and she made it boisterously obvious that she wanted me. Of course I was scared to death. Everyday after I ate my lunch, I had to walk right by her table of beautiful and attractive sisters. They would all stare me down in the most sensually intimidating manner imaginable as I struggled not to make eye contact and retain my composure. In my effort to appear aloof and uninterested, in hopes to assuage them to stop, I fueled the burning fire, and Tonya desired more. This cafeteria charade continued for several months and ventured beyond the confines of the cafeteria walls into the hallways during class transitions. I, being more accomplished with written words than verbal, decided to write Tonya a letter expressing my interest in getting to know her better on a one-on-one basis. This letter took refuge in my locker for several days, possibly weeks, before finally making it into the hands of its addressee.

During one of my classes, I asked to be excused to use the restroom, and while in the hall, I saw Tonya on the paralleling hallway about fifty yards away. I quickly gated forward, losing sight of her behind the row of classrooms separating the two corridors. I stopped and turned my back against the wall and listened to my heart begin to thud and rhythmically patter. I knew she had seen me and was headed my way, so I had to pull myself together, and quickly. I walked back towards the adjacent hallway and saw her; she was halfway to me already, and how convenient that this hall was where my locker was. The first things she asked me were if I had noticed her looking at me and if I had a girlfriend. I told her that I had noticed and that I didn't have a girlfriend, *and* that I had written her a letter. She smiled and then asked me if she could have the letter. I told her it was hers and of course she could have it but that it was in my locker. She looked disappointed, so I told her she was standing right in front of my locker and if she moved I could get it for her. She did move, and then she told me that she liked my style. This was comforting, especially considering that I was wearing plaid bellbottoms and a blue button up, red and white stitched 70's style shirt. I smiled, turned my combination, pulled the letter from the top shelf of my locker, and handed it to her. I explained to her that I needed to get to the restroom and back to class before we got caught, and she affirmed. After this, our trivial young fling began. This young woman took advantage of me in the worse way possible. I was young, naïve, gullible, and inexperienced. Although it was cool getting rides home from school with a senior (having an empty house for an hour before my parents returned from work) and sharing my music, clothes, and life with her, the association came with a fee. She played me. Tonya was involved with several other guys while she was involved with me. I heard stories of her drunken behavior in a hotel room after her prom; the prom that she claims to have solidified her date to prior to meeting me. I never saw any of the items I loaned her again, and without realizing it, I gave her a little of my dignity. Needless to say, the tryst had crashed and burned, and the once positive attention that I received from the association became embarrassingly alienating. However, I came into my own on one fine day when Kikotan was seized with a bomb threat. All students were dismissed and forced to evacuate under the blanket of 'early release day.' The in crowd students all went to a local restaurant for a quick bite to eat before dispersing to partake in their delinquent and worrisome task, neglecting all sobrieties. Then she approached me. Stacy Destromp, the princess of all that was skater, told me that my shirt was dope. I felt alive and appreciated again. After all of the careful deliberating and subsequent decision to wear plaid chinos and an old school collar, button up shirt, I could have been embarrassingly standoffish. After all, I had heard a slew of upper classmen laughing hysterically at me as I walked down the main hallway earlier that morning. But I flashed an acquiescent smile and said, "Thanks," while thinking, "she wants me."

Pooh was an albino looking Caucasian with whom I had Latin class. Because I was on the Latin, Math, and National Honor Society, Pooh thought it beneficial to take advantage of my fecund mind. He was not so much of a study partner, but his kleptomaniac mother would steal us alcohol if we gave her a ration for her troubles. I have no clue how Stacy knew Pooh, but somewhere in the crossfire of mutual friendship and coincidental timing, Stacy and I began hanging out at Pooh's together. On any given weekend night, there would be anywhere from four to twelve juvenile delinquents partaking in depraved acts in the name of youth and experimentation. We were free to do whatever we wanted to do at Pooh's; including personal exploration. For the record, it was rumored that Pooh could perform oral sex on himself, but I never stuck around to visually confirm his aptitude by means of notorious showcasing.

Most everyone developed a nickname. Mine was "Niggi Brox," which more than likely was homage to my skin color, or my will to get as jacked up as possible on any controlled or uncontrolled substance. Somehow, Stacy and I became inseparable. We began hanging out as friends; we would play hackie sack before school or go thrift store shopping after. Sometimes we would find the areas that had the weakest surveillance and smoke Marlboro Menthols on our lunch break. On the weekends we convened at (our now mutual friend) Pooh's house and smoked blunts and bong hits until we entered into delirium. Looking back on these times, I feel horrified for a myriad of reasons. I partook in some dealings that I am not proud of, and my priorities were screwed up, but the only person I let down was the future me. There are so many wonderful things I could have been experiencing. But somehow I know that God's design for my life is not flawed. Perhaps this period was a crossroad. In that case, I have been at the congregation of innumerous crossroads, and I have survived. Like many adults that I have crossed paths with on my journey, I have made excuses for my failure. This is ironic because I typically assume sole responsibility for my successes. But I noticed that I was trapped in this defeated cycle of blaming my past on my current insufficiencies. My truth is, as an adult, I am no longer able to play that card. Adults have got to accept accountability for their actions. Yes, we are all a product of our childhood, but the determination of our adult behaviors and decisions can either negate that past or follow in the same debilitating pattern of self-destructive incompetence.

Unaware of this wisdom, I was satisfied with my nickname, Niggi Brox, and continued to drink, smoke, and do whatever rebellious and delinquent acts I felt compelled to do. These experiences have hurt me; I have developed an addictive personality that will more than likely follow me to my grave. The bright side is that God's love and Christ's covenant with me will also follow me to my grave. Grace is always granted to those who desire redemption. When temptation calls and my will is weak, I pray that God will deliver me. He has and He will. I am loved. Among others, I have allowed these experiences to shame me. I should rejoice in the reality that God has granted me grace and mercy. I may be considered a black sheep in the eyes of Christianity, but His eye is always on the sparrow, black or not.

Let the Faux Good Times Roll

By the time I was sixteen and a junior in high school, I had built an unimpressive drug abuse portfolio ranging from ecstasy, marijuana, PCP, nitrous whip-its, cocaine, LSD, and hash, to of course nicotine and liquor. I thought my mode of social recourse was glorious. It was not until my therapy session some eight years later that I realized I was self-medicating and suffering from an addictive personality. The teenage boy's mind does not rationalize these things. An addict's mind does not rationalize these things. And that is exactly what I had become, a teenage addict. My hedonistic behaviors landed me an infamy around KHS; I knew how to party. I knew something was not right because my soul was dying and it was excruciating. I had one foot in the church and the other foot in the grave. I was occasionally attending St. Ignatius, but I had found more comfort in the contemporary confines of Campbell Temple. The drama department at Campbell performed the most magnificent musicals highlighting the life of Christ, Jesus. Afterwards, the pastor always lead an alter call and due to the catastrophic state of my life and perfunctory spirituality, I felt compelled to approach one evening. While under the hands of the prayer ushers, I felt ashamed. I remembered the little boy whose faith was so strong that he told his preschool classmates that he saw Jesus. I knew Jesus loved me; I had just sat through a two hour spectacular display that portrayed this and glorified the covenant that was made the day Jesus's last breath escaped his suffocating lungs on the cross. I began to cry and that made me feel alive. My soul was still alive! I gave my life to God and accepted His son, Jesus Christ, as my Lord and Savior. I connected with some of the youth at Campbell Temple and realized they lead more of an alternative lifestyle. I was intrigued, and I enjoyed the comradity. I felt an infusion of my hedonistic lifestyle and the one I was supposed to lead. I attended weekly youth groups, lock-ins, *Bible* studies, Christian concerts, and Sunday school. I was making new friends and changing my lifestyle... so I thought. I may have exercised sobriety and refrained from using foul language, but I was every bit the heathen I was prior to getting saved. My life had gone from just being an act to becoming a balancing act. As far as I was concerned, I was still dealing with the spiritually toxic affliction of being attracted to boys, and I was terrified that accepting this meant I was doomed to hell. I struggled to understand the equation man + man= hell; and if it were true, why me? I was still praying that maybe God would allow me to wake up one morning as a *regular* boy, with a *healthy* attraction to girls. I was still dreaming of that white picket fence and a beautiful family. My non-Christian friends had begun to sense that something was profoundly different in me, and I was afraid that if my Christian friends knew about my black secret, they would condemn me. I felt the most debilitating shame that ate away at me internally like an acid slowly devouring my organs. I tried to make an effort to remain friends if not civil to my social group while remaining devout to my spiritual group: It was a nightmare that played on repeat every waking moment of my excruciating life.

But suicide was not an option. I love myself way too much for that, and my mother did a pretty decent job of training me that suicide yielded instant hell, do not pass go or collect two-hundred dollars. So I continued to live my life of juggling things. I became quite a skilled balance actor actually. It was a lachrymose existence of fulfilling a role that society taught me it wanted me to be. Beyond the constant piercing pain and difficulties with duality faced on a daily social schema, I was also kept from being myself by the people who were supposed to love me unconditionally--my parents.

Perhaps it is a teenager's nature to mask pain by displaying behaviors that shock and baffle their parents. By this time (junior year), I had gone from wearing bajas and bucks to bleached blonde dreadlocks, jeans that were thirty-three inches wide at the ankle, chain wallets, rustic t-shirts, and piercings in my tongue and ears. But my act had backfired, I had become my parents little gimmick. They thought it was wonderful that I was a beneficiary of Dr. King's dream fulfilled. Members of their social network adored me because I was a record breaking competitive swimmer, an honor roll student, a talented musician, and a well-known social butterfly. Other teenagers seemed to gravitate towards me because I was unique, outgoing, rebellious, and party-oriented. It seemed I had found the answer to the equation for transferring heart-wrenching pain into success and popularity: faux good times.

I suppose I was a positive influence; there were very few people who truly knew me at this time. I could not understand why people enjoyed being friends with me. I felt that I had nothing special to offer anyone. My life was a joke; I was a clown acting in my own traveling circus. It was at this junction that I formed the ideology that having people think I was uniquely outgoing was better than them knowing the truth, and I would do anything to achieve this, including desecrate my body, dilute my mind, and poison my soul. Now I was already drug active, had been since fourteen, but I had not yet become sexually active. In fact, I would sometimes still entertain the idea of waking up straight and claim I was saving myself for marriage. I placed myself on a psychotropic drug hiatus and only smoked weed and drank alcohol. Sometimes I would get very paranoid while smoking marijuana, and now I understand why. I was concealing so many emotions that when I became high, it was uncomfortable to exist. But my reputation preceded me, and sobriety was not an option. It was only my few true friends who would understand who and what I genuinely was.

I do believe that friends are God's way of apologizing to us for our families (this is supposed to be funny, but it is actually quite sad). I do not entirely know when and how my friendships began. I can remember meeting my friends, but when the immeasurable love felt was cultivated remains a mystery. Friendships are important because they influence and support who we are as people. It is unlikely that an adult would become friends with a person they met in front of a gas station and dropped a bill into their cup; but the recipient of that bill may be the best damn friend in the world to an old man who is on the other side of town holding a sign at the freeway exit. Although a true friend will love and accept who we are regardless of class, culture, gender, and orientation, our class and culture can define us, and usually we become friends with people who understand us because they share a similar identity. As adults, I feel the major deficit inhibiting us from being friends with a vagrant is the cognitive inability to understand how one ever attains and sustains that state. For this reason, there is something esoteric about teenage friendships; I sometimes wish adults could sustain friendships of this same quality. Young people often befriend others out of the desire to be accepted, so we look to people who we feel are safe and will unconditionally accept us. Teenagers are also more skilled at compartmentalizing friendships. I would not have been comfortable at a rave with my friends from church. This code switching almost seemed natural to me, yet each relationship was equally as imperative to my maturation.

I had been swimming competitively since I was six, so my swim-mates represented a part of me that was athletic and wholesome. I joined the percussion ensemble when I was twelve, so my friendship with Deric represented the true test of transition, change, and understanding. Deric has always been a unique spirit, never one to assimilate, Deric marched to his own beat, and indeed, he played the drums. I met Carey and Linda through Stacy; they were what I called 'skater princesses.' They were exotic; Stacy and Linda were both products of biracial parents (Stacy being Japanese and Caucasian and Linda being Korean and Caucasian). I am not sure of Carey's ethnicity, but she was undoubtedly beautiful. She had deep auburn hair, chestnut eyes, and olive skin, but her physical appearance was not what made her gorgeous. Carey was a saint and willing to do anything for the people that she loved. Her best friend, Linda, was the same; loving and willing to do anything for her friends and family. The first night I hung out with these two, we became instant family. We took silly pictures, drank a bunch, talked, listened to the Beastie Boys and Deee-Lite all night, and drank some more. But this was all preliminary; I have done these things with acquaintances. It was the unconditional acceptance of each other that solidified our relationship.

Jay and I are so similar that it is rather humorous yet somewhat frightening at times. We attended the same preschool and middle school, some would attribute these random reconnections to the universe magnetizing our need for one another, but that would be undermining the true cause; God. Jay and I are soul mates, as my best friends and I tend to be. I believe that soul mates are often friends; some have a false understanding that this term exclusively refers to romantic relationships, but God has a way of making friendships sometimes feel more natural than familial and romantic relationships, which is why Jay and I constantly reconnected throughout our youth. God knew we needed each other. Jay and I were both raised under pretentious traditional values, but upon recognizing the damage caused by such materialism, we began to come into our own. Some may say that we rebelled, but I like to think of it as experimentation and exploration.

Jay, Stacy, Linda, Carey, and my girlfriend at the time, Shannah, were whom I considered to be my "inner-circle." On the second tier of the circle were Reba, Ronnie, Deric, and Christi. Jay, Deric, Reba, and I all went to middle school and were in band together. Jay and Deric were best friends in elementary school and somewhere upon the journey of middle school hell, we all connected and just became a little crew. Because we all went to a fundamental middle school, we went to different high schools. Ronnie became Jay's best friend that he met in his high school band; Deric, Christi, Stacy, Linda, Carey, Shannah and I all went to Kikotan. Deric and Christi were dating, and Linda and Carey were best friends who were both tight with Stacey. Shannah was a couple years younger than all of us but because she was my sweetheart, everyone loved her too. We were teenagers. We did teenager things. We talked about one another behind our backs. We got silly drunk and took care of each other when we consequently threw up. We skipped school, smoked cigarettes, attended concerts, went to Busch Gardens, had sleepovers, went to keg parties and clubs, rented hotel rooms, got in fights, and just plain grew up together. I have heard people say that if they had it all to do over again, they would do no differently, but I believe that I would. I would trade all of these faux good times for the knowledge that I was laying a foundation for years of turmoil and addiction. I know I had a friend in Christ; I could have been a light to a healthier, happier group of friends. But I chose to take the path of regret, which only yielded a sad story. This period of my life is not an entire regret; I actually can say that I chose a network of friends that legitimately loved and continue to love me. These people became my support system and my confidants. They took the place of the introverted brother who I had nothing in common with and the disconnected parents who were too concerned with their own lives and homophobic dispositions to listen to me. It may seem unfair to demand such an emotionally heavy consignment of teenage peers, but we provided this love for one another. In some internally disparaging manner, we were each other's support system, all providing the love a family needs to persevere, stay connected, and grow. I went to *The Tame* (Jay's, Ronnie's, and Deric's band) gigs when their parents were too busy; I helped Shannah with her homework when her divorcee mother was entertaining a friend, I was the shoulder for Stacy to cry on when relationships betrayed her, I was the ear to listen, the voice to give advice, and the heart that loved. But I was simply returning the favor for services rendered because all of the inner-circle residents had done the same for me. If it had not been for these friends, high school would have been even more so unbearable.

Towards the end of my time in high school, I became anxious to spread my wings. My ambition had superseded the buckling levies of Virginia Beach, and I was ready to break free. I had been accepted to Virginia State Polytech, which was not my first choice, but as God's will prevails, it turned out to be the most influential and developmental force in my life to date. I knew that when I left home to go to college it was going to be difficult not being close to the friends that I had come to know as family. But the script that God writes is like a river; one cannot control which direction the currents of life take them. I just pray that God equips and prepares me to stay afloat upon the current lest not be sunken under.

So senior year was about to end, I had the perfect relationship with Shannah, a network of friends who had also been accepted to Virginia State Polytech, including Deric's girlfriend, Christi, whom I adored. Things seemed to be headed in a great direction and how convenient because I had completely tired of Virginia Beach's narrowing and stagnant walls.

Fighting Gobbler Fever: Year One

It all happened so fast, my parents were unloading my things, and I was confirming my identity with the resident advisor and receiving the key to my residence for the next year, dorm room number 1004, Ditchard West. It was a bright and vibrant August day, and the new and returning students were out and about enjoying the beautiful Virginia State Polytech campus. The yard between Ditchard and PJ Halls was filled with chiseled, bare-chested Frisbee throwers, girls in their short shorts and halters revealing tanked waistlines and killer abs, tanning couples face down on their beach towels, and the sporadic loaners who brought their reading or music to occupy them between their spouts of people watching. Looking over the yard, I couldn't help but think, "JACKPOT!" Looking back at my mom, who was crying of course, and my dad, who was holding back tears of pride and relief, I did feel a faint discomfort. "What was going to happen to them now," I wondered? "Will they kill each other? Will they enjoy their empty nest?" I was young, and I did not care; I was free. I felt like Dorothy, only I did not want to go home. I hugged and kissed my parents goodbye and watched them drive off. The taillights of my mom and dad's sport utility vehicle got smaller and smaller until they became a blurred vision of red and green, and then my parents were completely out of sight, they had become 'just a phone call away.'

My roommate was no surprise at all; I decided to live with an old swim team buddy. Sabo and I did not have much in common, but we knew each other from home and the prospect of living with a total lunatic was not worth the gamble. In high school Sabo was hysterical, only he did not know it. He provided comic relief to every situation, whether another swimmer hyperventilated, or if a teammate missed their personal best by a quarter of a second, or if a final heat relay did not qualify for the Junior Olympic trials. Sabo and I also had been in several classes together and worked together on group projects. We worked well together, he allowed my creative dominance to shine and I needed his counterbalancing intellectual prowess. I decided to take advantage of Sabo arriving the next day by setting up my loft bed on the half of the room I felt most desirable. After I was settled, my neighbors introduced themselves; Andy and Will, two moderately attractive guys from Maryland, both Engineering majors. We played cards and drank cheap beer all night; it was the first time I actually felt like a teenager. I had been hiding for so long that it felt good to step out... but was spring finally here or would there be an eternal winter waiting? Who did these people expect me to be? Who did these people want me to be? Certainly not *a fag*, but the interesting thing is I was just me. They liked *me*.

My first year at Virginia State Polytech began with abundant partying. There was a starving white house with churning paint and neglected landscaping that was within walking distance from the dorm; it was appropriately called 'The Crack House.' Every Thursday night there was a keg party thrown at The Crack House by an unknown or specified host. Sabo, Andy, Will, and I would walk and once there, proceed to liquidate ourselves beyond measure. Of course extracurriculars were readily available, and we would occasionally partake, but for the majority of Thursdays, we just drank enough beer to diminish a barley and hops plantation. The events of these Thursday evenings were pretty much always the same, as if someone cloned the same party and put it on weekly repeat. The scene was overcrowded with drunks, smelt like an airport smoking lounge with a hint of micro brewery, and loud: always girls dancing, always guys preying, and never another person with my complexion, and somehow I felt safe here. I built up a tolerance to beer, by default, there was nothing other than Milwaukee's Best (aka Beast) to drink. I hated beer in high school, but these boys from Maryland taught me how to drink it out of a funnel and tube (beer bong), upside down out of the tap of the keg (keg stand), warm or cold (typical), and even room temperature with a cigarette butt floating in the can (trifling and too drunk to care).

By this time, Shannah and I had decided to just be friends. College was too overwhelming for me to sustain the relationship, and Shannah, crying on the phone, confessed that she had been feeling like I 'did not love her anymore' for a while. I cannot say that I was completely devastated by this news, as I was no longer in Virginia Beach and in a world that did not have a place for her. Shannah and I remain friends today and I love her every bit now as I did then. However, newly free from the monogamy of my first serious relationship, I began to explore and experience the fullness of life as a single male in college. One of the most coincidental occurrences of my freshman year, and perhaps my life, was discovering that a young lady that I had conditioned myself to be attracted to was the younger sister of a guy I would later become best friends with. Jillian and Jack Dubois and I shared an instant connection. Jillian was Christi's hall mate and close friend, and I frequently visited, went out with, and dined with Christi, and Jillian would often come along. During this period, I somehow became connected with a fourth year student by the name of Rachel May. She was glamorous in the same way Tonyagene was. Rachel lived off-campus, drove a new Toyota 4Runner, knew every bouncer at every bar and had no issues getting me in; it was like I was VPtech royalty. I was the freshman that everyone knew (probably because I was the only black male with blond dred-locks in the Shenandoah Valley), and wherever Rachel, Jack, and I were, was the place to be. I spent a majority of my weeknights with my freshman and campus locked friends, including Jillian. Jillian and I were attracted to each other and shared an innocent flirtation, but it never went further than a kiss. Rachel and Jack were friends previously, so she introduced me to Jack. Rachel or Jack would come and pick me up, and this allowed me to escape from my freshman life and enter into the world of sexual freedom and incantation of the eccentric Broxin. Off campus I could test the extent of how far I could push in disclosing my true self; whereas on campus, although I was liberated, I still felt a natural repression. Rachel urged me to be myself, in fact, she urged everyone to take their inner ambition to the max. She was a savvy opportunist, outrageous partier, and an astronomically skilled saleswoman; Rachel performed. Rachel and I fell in love with one another; however, I fell in love with her as a friend. We were such blithe spirits: magnanimous hearts: and gifted lovers of others. We recognized these socialite qualities within one another. We both were insatiable party animals and every bar, club, house party, and rave within a 3000-mile radius was fair game. Of course we made a name for ourselves around Brownsburg, but we wanted more than 1:30 last calls and 2:00 closing times. We began to drive to North Carolina, DC, New York, or anywhere, over any weekend for an all night party featuring every upper, downer, or all-a-rounder imaginable. Rachel was from a wealthy family, so money was not an issue. When presented with the prospect of more drugs, no was not a concern; and apparently in a world filled with psychotropic drugs, neither is a good reputation. I polluted my body with every drug I could get my hands on. It was ravenous; the irony is that these parties were referred to as raves.

Raving was not a total waste of time, I discovered I had an immense talent. Perhaps from the years of dancing with Stacey on Pooh's coffee table, or maybe at low-budget Richmond raves with Jay, Ronnie, and Deric, or even in Norfolk at some hole in the wall across the street from a Bank of America ATM; I had become a bad-ass dancer. I am not talking about booty shaking madness at the club, I mean I was amazingly good. I could take a song, beat, rhythm, or vocal performance during a break, and interpret its meaning through my limbs straight through my phalanges. When I was on the dance floor, people formed around me to witness the outward expression of joy, freedom, happiness, and celebration that I felt internally. I met so many fellow dancers just by hitting a soul groove and admiring their gift. My favorite music to date is Funky Breaks. Oh my goodness, I love it. I could dance all night. Unfortunately, there has always been a limited number of good breaks deejays. Where are they?

The gift of dancing became a tool. In the beginning I used this to express myself. This lead to capturing the interest of others, which lead to me feeling accepted by the attention and making friends, which lead to solicitation and acquisition of drugs. Unfortunately, the exploitation of talent does make one rich, (whether monetarily or in their desires) yet is quantitatively soul decaying. I never signed a deal with the devil, but I suffered from the terms of the contract all the same. This poisonous scene had become the lover of my soul, and although my heart had always belonged to Jesus, I placed Him in my book bag, along with all my vices. Jesus does not belong in a book bag, back pocket, top shelf, safe, cupboard, or diary. But I struggled, and I placed Him there, and for a very long time I took Him out precisely when I needed Him, and afterwards, I retired Him back into my book bag. In doing this, I let gravity rule my life. Gravity grounded me one particular occasion at a rather prodigious party in Raleigh, North Carolina, in the fall of 1997. I had managed to catch a ride with some friends I met through Rachel at VPtech to an annual rave party that I had attended in high school but always with my inner-circle and never with people that I had barely known. I rode down with Skylar (vastly intelligent, funny, morbid guy who was in love with Eva), Eva (chill, elusive, party girl from Virginia Beach who had a crush on me), and Terrill (Eva's gorgeous friend who was tragically hit by a car and killed while crossing the street some years later). I was particularly excited to be going to this party because I remembered that the venue was in an old closed down bank with underground safes. The safes were all internally connected creating somewhat of a labyrinth, each room containing a different genre of techno music. The main area, which I imagine was the atrium and lobby of the bank, housed the house deejays, and underneath, in the labyrinth, were the drum and base, funky breaks, trance, and trip-hop areas. I immediately made my way into the funky breaks room, having already taken an ecstasy pill, a microdot, a hit of LSD called black magic, and a few bumps of ketamine; I was feeling beyond myself. I remember dancing and experiencing an overwhelming feeling of love and happiness. I was grooving to funky breaks with some friends I met up with from the

Virginia Beach and Richmond party scenes. Everything was the usual mind altered fun and then suddenly, as if it was planned the entire time, the scene began to change before my eyes. My friends were all chanting, "Are you ready?" I was confused as to what they could be talking about, and so I responded, "Yeah, I'm ready." They all stripped their raver gear away to reveal eurodescent white robes. I felt as if I had died and gone to heaven, and subsequently, my hallucinations sustained this sensation. This was it; I had overdosed and gone to heaven. The white robes were only worn for a brief moment because shortly after I realized that heaven could certainly not be a dark room with funky breaks blaring in the background for eternity, my group of party friends morphed from angels by stripping their white robes to reveal black cloaks. And at that moment, I knew that I had overdosed, died, and gone to hell. I immediately turned around and ran towards what I thought was the exit of the room. It was the maze-like set up of the safes that would prove otherwise. I could not find my way out of the basement of the building. I ran from what sounded like one demonic asylum to the next, frantically searching for a way out. It did not help that my friends chased after me, in which I later found was an effort to calm me down, but at the time, I felt as if the chariots of Satan's rapturers were quick on my heels, and I fought with all of my soul to keep them away from me. After what seemed like an eternity but was probably only ten minutes, I found the ascension to the top floor where Africa Bambata was being featured as the premiere house deejay. I located Skylar, Terrill, and Eva, and disclosed to them what had happened, while unknowingly disclosing my unstable state of mind. They all comforted me for as long as what could have been endured before returning to the dance floor to exercise their desire to have a good time, while Terrill lingered to help me collect myself.

Terrill offered to give me a back rub, and hoping that my ecstasy would over power the LSD, I accepted. While Terrill complacently indulged in trying to stabilize me, I began to take notice of what was happening before my eyes. Demonic forces began to preclude my sane recovery and the entire scene before me changed from actuality into a cartoon, from the ceiling to the hardwood flooring of the old bank that we were presently seeking depravity in. My entire reality had transformed into a vision of color beyond natural means, things were loony and toony, and seemingly better than before, until Terrill positioned her head beside mine to ask if the massage felt good. I turned my head to answer, and I noticed that something was *not* cartoon-like about her appearance but actually more demonic looking. The strobe lights flashed to reveal Terrill's entire skull, sockets, nostrils, and mouth void of any life; I was erect with fear and within seconds, I left Terrill, Eva, and Skylar and would not see them again for the remainder of the weekend. I ran towards the entrance/exit and met a less than social bouncer who informed me that once I exited, reentrance was not possible without paying the admittance fee, and I gladly surrendered my habitation knowing that the last place I wanted to be was in hell. Once outside, realism returned to my vision, and the fresh southern breeze embraced me. I felt relieved. I walked a few minute steps and then sat up in the fetal position with my head in-between my knees and my back up against the abrasive brick of the old bank building. I was sobbing from fear and uncertainty and then I became conscious of a serpent like hiss approaching me. I looked up to see nothing, so I retired my head back to its comfort place amid my upright lap to notice the unsettling phiiisssst approach again. When I raised my head the second time, I noticed a janitorally clad middle-aged man sweeping the streets with a manila colored straw broom. This was reassuring to me, so I lowered my head again only to hear the hissing become closer and more menacing, and when I raised my head again, it immediately stopped, and the man scraped his toil into a black, flat dustpan. He was now only several yards from my feet, so I got up and walked southward on a destionationless journey away from Satan's grasps. I did not know where I was going, but I knew that I needed to get to safety, where Satan could not harm me. Where was such a place? I was not even convinced that I was still alive. The only place that I could go where I knew I could feel protected and alive was home, to Virginia Beach, Virginia. I decided to make Virginia Beach the destination of this drug induced journey.

As I walked the cobble-stone sidewalks, I passed many partiers who where engaging in drug exchanges and social anticipation of what was to meet them beyond the entrance into hell. Upon my journey, the first group of ravers that I met were empirical; absent of the edge a partier who truly understands drug induced stupors retains. I stopped to ask them for help, and the vacant looks upon their faces were communicating nervousness and rejection. I felt helpless and out of control, something like a vagrant soliciting help from others might feel. Realizing that the interchange was pointless, I abandoned this group and continued down the dark sidewalk. The next couple that I stumbled on seemed to be more approachable. They stopped to ask me if I was okay. Upon this exchange I realized that they were both mentally disabled. To my surprise when I spoke back to them, I discovered that I too was speaking in a garbled form of English. I was flabbergasted! Nothing was making sense auditorally, but mentally, I had no problems comprehending what was being said. It was bizarre yet reassuring, so I spoke to them a while. I realized that years of not understanding the communication I was subjected to while waiting for my dad to referee basketball games at Virginia Beach School for the Deaf and Blind made me somewhat of an intolerable prick. I could now understand that when I was disgusted by drooling individuals making incoherent gurgles at one another, that they were communicating in a manner that I could not comprehend; but now, for some reason, I could. I could not see my face, but I imagine that it was distorted similarly to the faces I was peering into: unlevel eyes, wide and uncontrollable mouths, and vacant expressions, indicative of a surface level of intellect and thought. I discovered that while this conversation was non-threatening, it was not helpful, and that I must continue if I were to escape the situation I was in. I felt that this benevolent couple was another of Satan's pawns sent to distract me from getting home to safety and love, so I abruptly ended the conversation and continued on my way. After taking a few more steps, my mind suddenly became oddly philosophical. I began to dissect political issues, social constructs, and leaders before my time. I was talking to myself aloud about solutions to world hunger, poverty, crime, and disease. I asked myself, "What would Martin Luther King Junior do in this situation?" I walked for a great distance in this state of mind before discovering an off duty cab parked on a corner. This was the omen that I had been anticipating! I walked around to the driver's side to see if he or she could give me a ride home and when the driver turned to face me, I saw that the entire right side of his face had been badly burned and his right eye was creamed over with a cataract-like absence of a pupil. My first reaction was, "Oh shit, it's Satan again!" But for some reason, I did not run away. I told him what had happened to me and begged his aid in getting home. He agreed to drive me to Virginia Beach (five and a half hours away) for around $400.00. He also told me that if he were going to be driving for this distance that he would need to pick up his brother for company on the drive. In hindsight, this seems like a preposterous engagement; I could have ended up murdered and never heard from again, but I was not of sound mind. In the state of mind that I was in, this sounded reasonable, so I accepted. The cab driver drove me to an ATM machine where I struggled for what seemed like an eternity to withdraw the funds because the letters and numbers on the screen refused to stand still long enough for me to press them. We drove to pick up the cab driver's younger brother and then we headed towards Virginia. From the backseat of the cab, I confessed everything that I had taken and explained what a rave party was. Both brothers listened quietly as I told them my story before commenting. They both agreed that I should refrain from keeping company with Caucasian people and cited that, "White people will get you into trouble every time and will never give a damn about you." Now, I do not believe this generalization to be true, but at the time of my hearing this, I agreed.

Over the course of the drive, I began to stabilize and become more coherent before finally arriving home. The brothers dropped me off, I thanked them, and I will probably never see either one of them again. I approached the front door and my heart was beating uncontrollably. I rang the doorbell and seconds later my dad answered. I was so overwhelmed at the sight of him in the flesh that I momentarily forgot how to breathe and collapsed. When I came to, I was lying down in the den on the couch, and my father was hovering over me with an expression of worry and confusion riddled through his forehead, eyes, and mouth. He asked me what happened and if I was okay. I told him. I explained that the only place I knew to come was home, and that I employed a taxi driver to bring me. In this conversation, I realized that not only was I alive but that I was also out of my mind! This perilous journey was nothing more than a drug induced, overdosed catastrophe. Nevertheless, I was home. It may have taken the sight of my father to believe that I was not in hell and alive and loved, so I was glad that I was home; and I believed it. After hearing what had happened, Dad immediately devised a plan. He told me to go upstairs to my room and shower and change while he arranged for me to catch a bus to Wilbursville, where Paul was attending the College of Virginia. Dad's main concern was getting me out of the house before my mother returned from church because she did not need to know that any of this had occurred. By the time I was ready, Dad had called the Virginia Beach bus station and gotten me a ticket to Wilbursville and called Paul and arranged for him to pick me up and take me to the Home Ride station. Home Ride is a college transit that stops at every large Virginian university, the first destination being William and Mary, then The University of Richmond, followed by the College of Virginia (CVA), then James Madison, Virginia State Polytech, and Radford. I had already missed the William and Mary stop, but I could catch the bus at CVA, where Paul was attending college, and ride back to Virginia State Polytech. It was a genius plan! While on the way to Wilbursville, I made the company of a Metallica loving masochist with a died onyx mohawk, several piercings, extensive eyeliner, painted black fingernails, too many belt chains to count adorning his stone washed Levi's, and combat boots. He was, at first, very apprehensive to talk to me, but being that our seats were adjacent and I was still high, I engaged in conversation with him. Eventually, he became enthralled by the amount of drugs that I had ingested and the sensation of feeling like I was being chased by Satan for hours. He asked for every detail with a look of amazement and disbelief in his eyes. He wanted to know if I was still tripping and what types of things I was seeing. I was thankful for him because talking about the experience helped my mind to come down from it. Before I knew it, the bus was pulling into the Wilbursville station, and I saw that Paul was frantically waiting for me. He took me to eat at one of the dining halls on campus, and we talked about what had happened. Paul and I prayed over the entire situation, and then he asked if I was involved with a church in Brownsburg. I told him that I was not. I could not remember the last time I had seen the inside of a church. And shortly thereafter, it was time for me to catch the bus back to Brownsburg. On the final leg of my trip, I debated going to church. I had marginally wanted to find a church, but life was happening so fast that I never did and made excuses for it. When I finally got back to school, there was a convoy of worried Fighting Gobblers posted vigil at my dorm room. No one had heard from me since I left the party. Sabo had been answering the phone non-stop with inquiries as to my whereabouts. Sklyar, Eva, and Terrill had called the hospital and police trying to find me before finally leaving Raleigh thinking the worst had happened to me, and I had to explain it all to them; the embarrassing and humiliating story of my overdose, flip out, cab ride home, and bus ride back to school. I have not touched a hallucinogenic drug since.

Looking back--fighting with my afflicted spirit, I abandoned God and Jesus completely. My desire to attend church had gone from marginal to non-existent, and the rules under which I learned about Christianity had become lost. There was a seed planted in my soul in desperate need of nurturing, however the circumstances under which my heart became toxic had caused me to become estranged from Jesus. I have encountered reprehensible betrayals as I have done things deserving of reproach myself. Supremely, no injustice is quite as devastating as those I have inflicted upon myself. Unknowingly, my mind has become a paper trail of repressed memories that manifest in a multitude of painful visions, unhealthy behaviors, and conditioned responses, and this trail leads directly to my heart. I would like to believe that I am an optimist, but my memories reveal that I am a cynic masquerading as an optimist who is truly an emotional masochist. To some degree, I never fully recovered from the pain of having dreams and parents who did not support them. I sometimes think of what type of person I would be if I had not spent so much time hating myself. I might be some wonderful author, or entertainer, or leader... God has not given up on my life and therefore, I should not either. And drugs, well they are just a false escape from pain and disappointment. Why alter a pleasant state? Being high provided release from the strains and pains of reality, and I had taken it too far. And God had sent me a clear wake up call.

> *I do not understand what I do. For what I*
> *want to do I do not do, but what I hate, I do*
> *(Romans 7:15).*

When I think of how many internal remorseful moments I have encountered, a heart wrenching pain shoots from my chest to my lower abdomen. When I have engaged in frivolity, I knew it was not the best for my spirit, although the self-indulgence was momentarily gratifying to my secularly desiring flesh. If it is true that we enter the world with a subconscious and innate desire to live in a manner that inflicts pain upon those who love us the most, imagine the pain due God who loves us unconditionally and with unfailing mercy and grace. I would like to think that God, being a force and not a being, does not contain a heart, but if he did, it would break every time his sparrows were lead astray. It is so important to protect your heart, because a broken heart is a paralyzing possession mainly for two reasons: My ex and I use to take annual trips to Florida at the beginning of each summer. Being that we were both teachers and on a budget, we would book our accommodations through travel agencies that promoted timeshare properties. With the commitment to tour a vacation property, one may earn amusement park tickets, several nights in a hotel, meal vouchers, and various other traveling perks. Our choice was the hotel accommodations, and prior to checking in one particular trip, we were very confident with the decision. Once inside of the room, we discovered mildew in the tub, rust around the shower knobs, hair in the sink, peeling wallpaper, holes in the dry wall, soiled stains in the carpet, broken furniture, filthy windows and bedding, inadequate lighting, and an overall inhabitable essence.

We slept in this room for one night, but complained so fervently during our timeshare tour (with digital pictures to illustrate the trifle) that we forged a relocation to the Radisson directly preceding our decision that we were not going to purchase a property from a company that would subject future residents to such detestable and abominable accommodations. The night at the Radisson felt like the Plaza compared to the previous. Analytically, a broken heart is debilitating because a heart is like a hotel room. Unfortunately, my heart was a filthy hotel room, instead of mildew and dirt, it was cluttered with wickedness and depravity. During my times of darkness, I was the furthest from Jesus. I do not believe that Jesus was not willing to check into my heart but that it was in such a reprehensible state that he could not comfortably take residence. The filthy accommodations of my heart needed to undergo major transformation so that I could offer Jesus the Radisson and not a Roach Motel.

The other reason a broken heart is toxic is more obvious. Metaphorically, if a heart is broken, it is not capable of fulfilling its secondary purpose which is to love. In order to free yourself to love, you must mend your broken heart. A heart may become broken in a variety of ways: a boyfriend/girlfriend may betray or hurt you, you may learn that a close relative has recently passed away, (and in my case) years of diabolism or hedonism can also leave a heart in a broken state. There is only one thing that has the power to mend a broken heart; a relationship with God. Through bittersweet reminiscing, I understand my first year at Virginia State Polytech to be a filed away epoch of my life. I endured copious joys and monumental heartache. The reality is that life can be incredibly easy to compartmentalize. The difficult part is finding what is important again. That is one of the many things that a relationship with God is good for.

Fighting Gobbler Fever: Year Two

My disgust at learning that my parents would not allow me to live off campus my sophomore year in college was beyond reproach. I was nineteen years old-a legal adult-yet still under the control of my parents. Presently, considering the astronomical amount of student loans I have remaining to pay, I should have politely told my parents, "Your opinions are futile," being much more polite than, "Go to hell." There is something harshly damning about the latter; I would not wish the eternal flames of the fiery pits of hell upon my worst enemies, so considering saying that to my parents should attest for how badly I wanted to live off campus. While I was requesting 1004 Ditchard West on the on-campus-residence form, every person I knew at Virginia State Polytech was signing a year lease for their new strategically chosen apartments. It was like involuntary alienation of the worst kind. I was terrified; would I have the same luck making friends with the new upcoming freshmen? Rachel had graduated, so I couldn't depend on her for social networking. Thank goodness for Jack, and thank goodness for Kookie. Out of all the vehicles I have ever owned, Kookie is the dearest to me. Kookie Kiara: a

1997, champagne colored Kia Sportage that my parents purchased for me the summer between my freshman and sophomore years. It was the first thing that had ever entirely belonged to me. I did not have to share her with Paul, her appearance and longevity were solely dependent upon me, and she reciprocated in her dual responsibility; I could come and go as I pleased, thanks be to Kookie. My roommate on the other hand was a travesty. I believe his birth given name was Carlisle, but all of his friends called him Egon and he was ok with it. I called Egon before we were due to arrive to discuss who would bring what. I had a stereo, microwave, and television, all he had to bring was a refrigerator. I could tell through our telephone conversation that I would be spending as little time in the dorm room as possible. Egon was completely socially inadequate and somewhat bizarre. At the end of my sentences I was told, "Cool," no matter what I previously said. I *could* have said, "I am a raging homosexual and will be having lots of gay sex in our dorm room," only to be received by a Beavis and Buttheadesque, "Cool." It almost sounded as if it should be spelled K-U-I-L-E. He was a mess; instantly upon meeting him, I knew that he had spent more time in front of the computer than on the phone, or in the mall, or at a party, or hell, even masturbating. Not that these things are the only acceptable practices for teenage boys, but typing on the computer and going to class hardly makes one well rounded. Egon rarely left our Ditchard Hall dwellings, and I came and went so frequently that my schedule would have permitted some sporadic chance of him at least eating. Perhaps the reason I did not come home while he was dining is for the simple fact that he believed he was a vampire. Yes, he would tell me about the many vampires on campus. The vampire society convened at night in an undisclosed location and did whatever it is that vampires do. Please note that there was one missing persons report filed at Virginia State Polytech between the years of 1997 and 2001. Certainly a true vampire would need to feast more than once in four years. In my attempt to understand what being a vampire meant and to ensure Egon was not thinking about feasting on my blood in my sleep, I asked him about his alternative lifestyle. Apparently, being a vampire is not solely dedicated to the plasma-thirsty bloodsuckers. In fact, anyone who wanted to become a vampire could simply by abandoning their reality and adopting a new identity. I thought, "Hell, I suppose I've been a vampire for the greater portion of my life." I can't say that I blamed Egon for wanting to masquerade as a... whatever his mind ventured to. I wondered, was he comfortable once returning to reality? If so, why escape? Well, one night while I was trying to sleep, I heard my answer. Imagine the sound of a keyboard being violently manipulated with pauses in between. It was 3:00 am and Egon was engaged in a lovers' quarrel with his cyber girlfriend. It occurred to me that they had never met one another in the flesh due to the Geisha themed photograph that this undeniably white girl had taken of herself in which she was fully made up in traditional Chinese concubine kimono and face paint. I wondered what image she was presently looking at of Egon. They were both very much involved in a reality relationship that was being sustained by whatever character they thought the other wanted them to be. His reality was a farce; he had been escaping a majority of his life as well. Egon never returned to reality because *his* reality incorporated the nonsense right into it. This is when I decided that I needed to leave this dorm room as often as possible, it was too familiarly oppressive. So I began to spend a significant amount of time at Christi and Jillian's apartment. They had a third roommate, Anne, and we were a little family of sorts; Anne (Banana), Jillian (Bean), Christi

(Stina), and Broxin (Crackhead). I liked being with Christi because we had known one another throughout high school, Deric visited frequently, and Jillian intrigued me with her northern Virginian snobbery and vast knowledge of mindless, yet socially superior etiquette. She, in a way, taught us all about how to extract only the superlative elements of Pop culture and utilize them to become extraordinary. I began to fall in love with her taste in music and food, knowledge of celebrity gossip, relentlessly mindless television, and vegetation on the couch while indulging in these shows and being totally pampered by beautification aids. I suppose she was my "propriety liaison." She and Jack were so different. He was full of knowledge as well, equal in caliber to Jillian's, but entirely different in type. Most everything Jack knew about the world he had learned through observation and/or reading from a more scholarly source. The two were a perfect sibling pair; Jack did Jillian's homework when she became burned out by academic overstimulation as Jillian would tell Jack when and how his outfit, hair, or life was a mess and how to fix it. While Jillian was teaching me how to apply concealer to acne, Jack was teaching me how to maximize seduction through channels of social interaction, non-verbals, and mannerisms. Life was seemingly wonderful my first semester, second year, until I went home for Holiday Furlough. It was back to Virginia Beach again for Christmas cheer and high school debauchery revisited. I do not recall much from that break, but the part that I do recall landed me in the hospital. Jay, Stacy, Deric, and I decided to spend my last night at home before driving back to VPtech at a friend's house-party in Richmond just off of Virginia Commonwealth University's campus. Of course we were smoking, drinking, and behaving recklessly when we overheard some drunken harangue resonating from the street. We all dispersed onto the front porch to see two random frat boys arguing over some act that was done prior to our overhearing the root of the argument. The host of the party we were attending, KC, decided to step out onto the lawn to try to remove the altercation from his property when one of the frat boys swung on him, turning a verbal incident into what would become a physical calamity. In an effort to defend himself, KC began fighting back. The frat boy ended up getting beaten up pretty badly, but it was not an entire victory for KC. Within seconds, a swarm of frat boys came running out of their neighboring house and began to jump KC. It was a nightmare. Most of KC's friends who were witnessing the incident all ran out into the lawn to help him. Watching from the front porch in total shock and terror, I realized that I was watching a brawl that was not going to be ended on pure merit and that the police needed to be called. I used my cell phone to call the police and did my best to figure out what the address was and to describe the severity of the situation. Things were escalating quickly and then they went from bad to worse. Stacy decided that she was going to go out into the brawl and do something about it. I say, "Do something about it," because I have not a clue what was running through her mind. I do not understand how someone her size (5'2 and 100 pounds dripping wet) could think that she could have done *anything* to stop what was happening. So of course she got assaulted and pushed down within seconds. I turned to look at Jay with, "We have got to do something," written in my eyes. Jay looked at me with, "I am not going out there," in his. So, I did the unthinkable and in hindsight, very stupid thing; I went out to rescue Stacy from the lion's den. The next thing I remembered was a haze best illustrated by cartoon characters that have been violently struck by some insane object on the head. I literally saw spots; I had been hit, a violent blow that had left me in a dazed state of consciousness. Stacy and

Deric dragged me from the midst of the brawl and we waited around for the police. I remember being in excruciating pain and feeling like my jaw was hanging onto my skull by skin and flesh. The police arrived and took statements, and after some arrests were made, we all drove home.

The next morning, my mother made a great breakfast and was sending me off to school in her typical fashion. I had heard my mother talk of her mother's intuition, and I had formulated my own opinions on the validity of her self-proclaimed innate and infinite knowledge of her children. This particular morning was the last day that I questioned any such motherly omniscience, for she took one look at my eyes and my inability to chew the scrambled eggs she had prepared with love and knew that I needed to see a doctor. Mom drove me to the emergency room, and the next morning I was entering into emergency oral surgery to correct my fractured jaw.

I have Stacy to thank for the plate and bolts that will remain in my face until I die. Perhaps a thank you is also due for the valuable lesson she taught me, however it is one that carries the utmost bitterness due to the wastefulness of the entire situation. Through my injury, I had hoped that Stacy would have learned a lesson, yet she still remains ridiculously too big for her britches. I shall never fight another one of her battles again.

After returning to school, Christi, Jillian, and Anne agreed to allow me to stay with them until I was well enough to go back to the dorms. This was the most magnificent time I had at Virginia State Polytech to date. Stina, Banana, Bean, and Crackhead became a family unit, and I attribute all of my knowledge of domestic sufficiency and cleanliness to living with these three young ladies. I was not really a crack-head in the literal sense, this became my nick name for actions such as the Pterodactyl swoop; hovering over an unsuspecting diner's plate while identifying the prey most appetizing before removing it in a swift, swoop-hook-like motion. The four of us shared many laughs while getting ready for classes, or watching a movie, or studying. But like all things in life, it had to come to an end. After I got my wires removed and began eating solids, I was back in the dorms and pondering over how I was going to gain all the weight I lost back. My answer came in a package named Tate Hampton. He had also suffered from a calamity that caused his entire body to be muscularly reconstructed. Tate was anatomically correct and patronized the gym in order to perpetuate this fortunate physical state. I met Tate while dancing at a techno club and being that my skills still attracted many spectators, Tate gestured at licking his pointer finger and placed it on my neck making a sizzling noise, implicating that I was hot. I am assuming Tate intended to mean my dancing, but I thought he was sizzling hot without the dancing. Tate and I became friends and due to his unfortunate accident, he understood my desire to achieve post surgical physical perfection. Tate and I became weekday workout buddies and weekend party buddies. Although Tate and I never crossed the friendship line, I did tell him that I was gay and he did not seem to allow that to affect our friendship. I met a majority of his friends, including his girlfriend, and became a "little brother" caricature in his life. His girlfriend, Natalie, did not seem to mind our friendship either; she was always so kind and supportive of our relationship. The greatest shock about Tate's character was that he enjoyed doing drugs as much as I did, so we often incorporated them into our weekend festivities. Appearing at off-campus gatherings, bars, and clubs incited a myriad amount of gossip. People intriguingly questioned me about how Tate and I cultivated a friendship, had we crossed the friendship line, and why we were friends. Surprisingly, the gossip did not bother him, and I no longer was as crazy about him as I first thought I was. Subsequent to our strenuous work outs, seeing him preparing for the shower or lounging around bare-chested was hardly a turn on. Tate had entered friend territory, and I loved him as such. So nearly a semester later, I was thirty pounds heavier, six percent body fat, and more popular than ever before. Tate graduated that year, and I never heard from him again, but I thank him for his role in my discovery of the gym and muscular perfection.

Fighting Gobbler Fever: Years Three and Four

Towards the end of my last semester at VPtech, I had interviewed several prospective roommates. I found the perfect match, three straight guys from northern Virginia; Scottie, Sky, and Armo. They had all gone to high school together and were looking for a fourth roommate in a two-story townhouse in the Phissher Run community. Jillian was friends with Armo, so she is ultimately responsible for the alliance, but I gave a buzz-worthy performance on my interview, having had an entire semester to buff up for the role and perfect my ongoing heterosexual masquerade. The townhouse was a dream, huge with a built in projector in the living room, built in bar with kegerator in the entertainment room, foosball table, eat in kitchen, back deck, and upstairs bed and bathrooms. Because Scottie was an Engineering major and they all had money, these items were not only easily built by skilled hands, but also easily obtainable. Our house was also incredibly diverse; Scottie was Caucasian: Armo was Armenian: Sky was Asian. Of course I made up the Black quotient of the United Colors of Phissher Run, as we called ourselves.

I became close to all of these fellows, but undeniably the closest with Sky. He was definitely concerned with appearances and social aptitude. We shared the same major, so we were often in the same classes, allowing us to car pool. Scottie was a Christian and (thank goodness) clean because I shared a bathroom with him. I also enjoyed talking to Scottie about our faith; he was effortless to talk to and unintimidating. Armo was the Alpha male of the house and went by Armo, paying homage to his Armenian roots. Although he was a man's man, he was not intimidating. Armo cared about his friends and wanted everyone around him to always be enjoying themselves, hence being the roommate who frequently suggested throwing parties in which our place would be packed to the max with people. The parties were a blast, but we all enjoyed going downtown more than anything. Drinking was not always a certain thing, as I was still twenty and the influence of Tate and Rachel no longer available to me. Armo was cool with a few bouncers who would let me slide, but their shifts were unknown and my admittance with an over twenty-one wristband not guaranteed. I lived with these guys for my last two years at VPtech. I never came out to them, but I am sure they knew I was gay. This had to have been confusing to them because I had more heterosexual sex than the three of them combined. The beginning of my Phissher Run of sex was with Christi. We happen to be in the same philosophy lecture and lab and began to study together. Sometimes I would study over at the Pink Palace, and on several occasions she would study at Phissher Run. Due to the rigor of the class, we would often study late into the evenings until we were utterly exhausted which resulted in sleepovers. One particular morning, I was awoken by Christi kissing my cheek and neck. Somewhere in between sleep and consciousness, I found myself becoming very much aware of my morning erection. Other than hormones, I cannot be too sure of what exactly came over me, but I turned her over onto her back and had intercourse with her; rough, passionate, and to climax. Surprisingly, I enjoyed it, and she did too. But I had crossed a forbidden line and broken the most common of friendship rules by sleeping with the ex of one of my best friends, Deric. The first person I told was my mom; she immediately voiced her disgust in my poor decision, expressing her emotional hypothesis that she would not be surprised if Deric never spoke to me again. I spoke to Christi, my roommates, Jack, and Jillian about this in great depth. Every conversation had the same conclusion; that Deric needed to be made aware of this situation. Disclosing the occurrence may have been avoided if it had been an isolated incident, but because Christi and I developed a very comfortable courtship, it was the universal opinion that Deric needed to be told. So I told him. To my surprise, he responded that he had always known that it would happen and that it was just a matter of time. I asked myself how could Deric have known this would happen years ago and Christi and I not have a clue? I feel it is because he truly knew and loved both of us and was extremely aware of the fact that once the connection he provided between the two of us was removed, we would cultivate one of our own, and this connection would be remarkable. It has been a while, but I used to contemplate that if I were not gay, perhaps Christi would be my wife.

Christi became sort of the den mom at Phissher Run. Her consistent female presence amongst four young men made her compulsion to clean, cook, and nurture welcomed and appreciated. I suppose it was nice having a girlfriend too, although as I mentioned, my roommates were probably confused beyond understanding, but this is appropriate because I was too. I could not understand how I was able to become aroused by not only a female, but Stina, my friend. And another interesting fact was that I could not maintain my arousal unless she was beneath me in the missionary position. Maybe I had finally given in to what I felt society's expectations of me were. I knew I was not straight, maybe I really was bisexual. Christi and I lasted for roughly a semester before eventually fading back into a plutonic friendship, which faded into nothing at all. From that relationship, a series of encounters with girls happened to me resulting in my roommates naming me Broxin Panty Toxin Mackle Model Delano Jingle Heimer Smitt. Females downtown accosted me on numerous occasions asking me if I were a model and if I had a girlfriend. It was simultaneously thrilling, flattering, and uncomfortable. Things being uncomfortable were in short attributed to the big, black secret that I was hiding; my attraction to men. Yet, I had never been with a man sexually. I needed to end this uncertainty immediately, and so I did.

Virginia State Polytech played Florida State in the 2000 Sugar Bowl, and it was in Nola, Louisiana that I lost my, what I call, bunghole virginity. A mutual lesbian friend of Jack and mine, MD, drove down to Louisiana for the grand event. Of course MD went to actually see the game; Jack and I went to actually see the men. We read that there were full on male strip clubs in Nola, total nudity, and a red- light district on Whiskey Street. I had never seen so many young people acting so foolishly. It was like Mardi Gras without the beads. I told myself that I was going to have sex with a man on this trip. I figured I might as well see what all of the hoopla was about. I do not remember much of the experience as I was completely wasted and just trying to have it. The man was quite a bit older than me which is gross looking back on the situation. I would guess him *at least* forty, to my twenty-one. I met him at Oz, a gay strip club/bar and lounge on Whiskey Street. He was reasonably attractive and to him, I am sure he found me to be a confused college kid. We both knew quickly that we wanted the same thing, so we walked back to his condo off Whiskey Street and had sex. I remember this man having a tattoo of a dolphin on his right ankle but other than that, he is just some man out there in the world who will forever have a part of me; it's disgusting. Although, this experience was meaningless, crude, and self-destructive, I find it similar to the way the Old Testament describes sexual acts. The only difference is a great Biblical character was not conceived upon my deed. I birthed a monster. From that night, I have been chasing a good sexual encounter, one that would be gratifying and loving. How foolish of me to search for gratification and love externally. So I went back to school emptier than I left and with a rancid memory of my man-on-man virginity forever gone. I was now a homosexual.

Shortly after the Sugar Bowl, Paul came to Virginia State Polytech for a Christian concert and seminar. Paul called and told me he was coming with some of his friends from church and that I should meet them there, so I did. The performance was poignant for two reasons; I was thrilled to see that Paul had forged true friends and found a strong and genuine relationship with Christ, and I had my first fellowship since I had been at Virginia State Polytech. Paul seemed to be extremely interested in my salvation and wanted to ensure that I found a church home and small group to keep myself connected to God. I promised that I would start reading my Bible again and attending the Campus Crusades for Christ (CCC) church and I did. The first book that I decided to read after my weekend with Paul was Romans; it was magnificent. I felt as if Paul (The Apostle) was speaking directly to me. I was moved to tears of overwhelming joy to discover the love that Jesus and God have for me despite my sexual preference. My path has been rocky, yet through the grace and mercy of God I have been forgiven. I am not alone in this joyous amnesty. God loves us all and forgives us all despite what anyone says.

Then I began attending CCC every Sunday and the more involved I became, the more I began to question my relentless attraction to men. It seemed as if Christianity and Homosexuality were incompatible, and I felt like I was caught in the crossfire. I did not know what I was going to do. I knew that no amount of prayer could remove the desires I harbored to have a man kiss and hold me. The incessant feeling of self hatred is impossible to overcome when you are being told that God created you in his image, makes no mistakes, and also hates homosexuals. I believed the latter and I began to hate myself as well. How could it be that God hates anything, isn't God synonymous with love? I may not be the most righteous person, but I have loved the Lord since the day I saw him fly across my preschool playground, and I was just as gay spirited then as I am now. Jesus loves me just as much now as he did then.

Attending CCC introduced me to an entirely new subset of friends which caused some rifts in my old group of friends. People did not understand how I could be a member of a religious organization that preached that I was damned to hell. This is a debate that is not mine to have. The Bible states that sexual depravity such as sodomy is sin. Does this excuse lesbians from the eternal fires of damnation? What about the heterosexuals who enjoy their anal hanky panky? The Bible states that a man lying with another man is sin and punishable by infinite suffering in hell. Does this mean that someone with a heart for Christ and faithful devotion to the Lord will suffer in hell because they happen to be in love with someone of the same gender? I asked why? Why would God make these senseless rules? I do not believe that God did. There is so much in the Bible that people choose whether or not to interpret literally. Some do not even believe Jonah was really swallowed by a whale. I personally do. So tell me it is not possible, then define miracle. It is certainly possible for the same God who resurrected a man from death to keep a man in the belly of a whale for three days. The Bible bids slaves to honor their master. Slavery is perhaps the most inhumane practice ever to be carried out. Forcing another being to abandon their personal freedom while subjecting them to an ongoing torture so grossly disturbing that it engendered massive suicides and still traces of the debilitating prejudices are evident in our modern culture sounds like God's word, *really*? In my experience, the Bible serves as a guide to life. The word has been interpreted, translated, and passed down for many centuries. I will not have the answers to everything, and I choose to admit this reality rather than pass judgments and argue. I allow my heart and soul to interpret what my mind cannot. Jesus dwells within my soul, so my interpretations are seldom without divine intervention.

A Temporary Place to Call Home

I graduated from Virginia State Polytech with a Bachelor of Science degree in the fields of Sociology and Criminal Justice. My desire to leave Brownsburg was similar to the anxiety I felt when I was craving exodus from Virginia Beach. The irony is that I ended up back in Virginia Beach. I moved in with my parents for eight months as I trained with my very first job out of college, Enterprise Car Leasing.

My first day at Enterprise was September 11, 2001, a particularly gorgeous day in Virginia until it became the day our country was seized by the most barbaric terrorist attacks in American history. I have often heard people describe the day they heard about Kennedy's assassination or Japan's attack on Pearl Harbor, it seemed so cliché. Each account was prefaced with, "I can remember it like it was yesterday: exactly where I was, what I was doing, what I was wearing…" Recounting this day is an initiation into this reminiscent society because I remember it as if it were a scene from a favorite movie rewound and continuously replicated over and over and over again. For those who remember this day and witnessing the footage on the news, it was like watching the special effects in an action film. It was devastating and grossly disturbing. Virginia Beach is surrounded by military bases, United States Coast Guard, Navy, Marines, Airforce, and NASA, so our branch's fleet was completely depleted due to the amount of military renting anything with four wheels in order to make it to Washington DC. I bypassed all training and learned the ropes directly from the wolves I had been thrown to this hectic yet beautiful Fall day. I was already bitter because the company's policies required that I cut my dred locks that I had spent over five years growing, but when I got home and watched the bodies falling from the World Trade Centers on the news, I felt even more disgusted and angry. Perhaps I associated this travesty filled day with Enterprise or maybe it was the hair. Whatever the disconnect, I knew I would not be retiring from the car leasing business, yet Enterprise would be my ticket to an enterprise beyond Hampton Roads. In the interim, I would save money and gain experience and seize the next opportunity to move on. This was wonderful because I was able to keep company with all of my friends from high school as I saved up enough money to move. Also during this time, I was able to develop a respect for my father that I did not feel I would ever be capable of achieving. I came to understand the toils of his life in dealing with my matriarchal mother and her *Type A* personality. I learned that my father is a submissive man with subdued traits and somewhat of a sleeping giant. The doctor's diagnosis of Type II Diabetes had drastically limited his ability to consume fermented alcohols, which are essentially all alcohols. Dad was two years shy of retiring and mostly just wanted to be left to his own vices of watching repeat westerns on TNT, which garnished great censure from my mother: visiting his buddies in Tarboro, North Carolina, which garnished great censure from my mother: eating comfort foods, which garnished great censure from my mother: and trying to enjoy himself in any way that would not garnish great censure from my mother, which garnished great censure from my mother. Our breakthrough bonding moment was spawned when my parents were entertaining their poker friends one Friday evening as they ritually did most weekends. My mother, displeased that I had consumed more alcohol than she thought necessary, began to censure me in a relentless tirade, regarding my level of liquor intake as common and my behavior as even more base. I am not one to retaliate to unsolicited, judgmental criticism with a slight tongue, so I informed her of the obvious objectives: I was twenty-one years old, the legal drinking age, and in the safety of my own home under the supervision of adults including the proclivity of my parents. With this truthful assessment of the situation and flagrant attempt to shut my mother down, she became belligerent at the responses of agreement received by her guests. Hopeless and unequipped, she rebutted with an open invitation to leave her home... so I did. Unfortunately, due to the level of intoxication that I had reached, it was not a quiet migration. I proceeded up the stairs to my bedroom in a fit of amateur adult liberation and began packing by tossing dresser drawers around as if they were junk mail received after a long day at work. My father knocked on the door and asked me to take a walk with him...so I did, much quieter than I had been packing. We walked around the block, and on this midnight stroll I discovered how very much we ironically had in common. We have both been raised by a woman who has conditioned us to: never question her, always temper ourselves to respect her feelings, never expect an apology from her, accept her opinions as our own, and do her will. The ironic component is that I had no choice but being raised by this woman, however, my father had chosen to marry her and bend to her will as a son often does for his mother. Dad told me that although he understood my frustration and behavior, it would work no hardship on my mother because she was too prideful. My father also disclosed that he had learned not to argue and to accept her rulings because the road to opposition had gotten him nowhere in his twenty plus years of marriage. I could not help but to see the disappointment in his face, but it was a disappointment that was overwhelmed by love. I told him how unfair I thought it was to be in a marriage and have to suppress true estimations. My father disagreed with me citing that he knew when to and when not to bend and an episode such as what transpired between my mother and I was not the appropriate time to resist. I asked him what he thought I should do, and he told me that instead of fighting her with words and emotion, to fight with actions. If moving out is what she wanted than that is what I would give her. It was in this moment that I realized that I had pegged my dad as the enemy for years and presently, he was the only one who understood. It was a new dawn in which the sun had risen on a cloud of forgiveness. Imagine someone you love very much telling you that they have a surprise for you. Now imagine this individual bringing you to a storage unit and inside…behold all of the items you have ever lost in your life. Whether it be a childhood wallet or security trinket, or an adult watch or piece of jewelry, or even replaceable items like chap stick or that twenty dollar bill you swore you left in your sock drawer, or maybe even thousands of dollars lost on a foreclosed home or plummeted stocks… Every single tangible object you have misplaced or lost here in this room, collected and kept safe since the day they exited your life. I imagine this feeling being equivalent to the way I felt after this eye-opening walk with my dad. Furthermore, I imagine this feeling being multiplied by infinity the day I meet God. Until then, all lost items are gone, and earth is just a temporary place to call home.

I decided this night that I needed to move out to a place I could permanently call home. The severe intimidation of this realization was that this place would not be the grey area determined by the co-dependence of a college campus, but a place free from parental control and entirely self-established where I paid bills, worked for a living, and least importantly, where *I* determined how much alcohol was suitable to consume.

Fortunately, Jack had moved to Terminus immediately following graduation. I had visited him more often than I realized had cultivated a deep love for the city. So, on April 1, 2002, I packed a U-Haul, Kookie, and my parents Expedition, and headed south. Nine hours later I pulled up to the front step of my very first apartment, 889 Vedado Way, # 2, Terminus, Georgia.

Terminus

"**S**avannah would be betta fo'ya! You'd just get into trouble in Terminus." I kept hearing Mammie's words taunting Scarlett. But how could this be the case for me? I didn't need to heed Mammie's warnings... Enterprise had transferred me to the Elkhead location, I had over $3,000 in the bank, and my parents had come to help move me in, so obviously granting me their blessings. Rubbish. I cried like a newborn when my family hugged me goodbye. There was no longer any more comfortable grey area, and I was on my own. I suppose I underestimated the reality of having every moment I saw my parents for the rest of my life just being a visit having such an emotional impact. It had become a bon voyage, Mom, Dad, Paul, Aunt, and Ollie were all there to wish me well in my new home. When we hugged goodbye, I felt scared. It is not the type of fright that one may experience after watching a scary movie or before a meeting with their boss, but more of an uncertainty of what is to come and knowingly having to face it alone. I was terrified by my hypothetical adult realities. I remember hugging my Aunt last and seeing tears welling up in her eyes, I began to cry. It was uncontrollable, and the more I fought back the tears, the more powerful the urge of catharsis became. So there I stood, watching the taillights of my parents green Expedition becoming a blur, but this time the blur was because of my tears. I now understood Dorothy's longing for home.

Crying, I called Jack for some degree of comfort and empathy, and he mockingly said, "Boo hoo, get over it! Now it is time to perform sista." There was no level of understanding for the tremendous fear I was enduring, only a desire to be young, gay, and fabulous. Jack was a monster indeed, but I quickly dried my tears and joined him on his gorgeous journey to satisfy his monstrous appetite. Undeniably, Savannah would have been better for both of us. My drug sobriety and church attendance were both gone with the wind.

Jack and I first began patronizing Blues, a gay circuit club on Summer Street in midtown. We were the perfect clubbing duo because we loved each other, yet we were social enough to go our separate ways and meet other guys. I had received great acclaim for the time I spent in the gym perfecting my anatomy, and Jack enjoyed more of an intellectual stimulation by the conversation that took place in the lounge area. I was reunited with the dance floor, except this time I was not achieving a soul groove because of my love of the music or to make friends, I had but one purpose; to seduce. I learned how to use my waistline as a rod, my chest as bait, and my smile as the hook to lure a man in. Jack and I habitually partied at Blues until they closed, then headed to Frontstreet and partied some more. Frontstreet was open twenty-four hours and because Terminus's gay circuit scene was at its prime, it was an exciting and abundant arena for Jack and me to play. Being fairly new to Terminus and therefore mysterious, I became completely misguided with absurd priorities. We discovered that by creating a breathtaking effect using John's intellect, eyes, and lips, and my smile, pecs, and waistline, we could obtain drugs absolutely gratis. And we did. We were superheroes in a sea of civilians who did not stand a chance against my body karate and Jack's sensuality. Jack and I took turns soliciting the acquisition of drugs, he would send me on my way taunting, "Give em sex Broxin," or, "ugh uh, sistah, take your shirt off. Okay, okay, now go!" Jack and I coined the phrase *sexualizing* to represent this barbaric behavior that combines socializing and imploring overtly sexual behavior for the purpose of solidifying sexual partners and/or drugs. Sexualizing was stimulating and effortless to me. I was six percent body fat with a thirty-one inch waist and forty-two inch chest. I was ridiculously in shape (physically) and used this to my advantage.

At this juncture of my life, I was able to count on two hands the number of men *and women* I had been intimate with. Then I fell in love. I met Dr. Greg at Blues and approached him much like I approached many of the men I met there. I was bare-chested, sprinkled with sweat, and had every zit on my face concealed to perfection. Dr. Greg was standing alone, arms crossed and with a look of voyeuristic dissatisfaction on his chiseled and beautiful Middle Eastern face. I asked him why he looked so unhappy, and he glanced my way. He was obviously pleased with what he saw, yet the gay male ego does not easily portray these internal thoughts. Dr. Greg asked me what I meant, so I coyly said, "You are standing in a hopping club in one of the best cities in the country, *and* a really attractive guy just came over to talk to you, the least you could do is smile." And he did. The rest of the conversation was textbook: where are you from, what do you do, how long you been in Terminus… We exchanged numbers and made tenuous plans to get together the following evening for dinner. And we did.

Dr. Greg and I sat at an intimate yet well lit table for two at Aprez Diem, and it was on this first date that he informed me that he had resigned from his practice in the city and gotten a job with an ear, nose, and throat practice in Lexington, Kentucky. The deal was done, the ink dry on the paper. "Damn," I thought! Graciously accepting his fate, I told him that we could still be friends and he agreed entirely. Dr. Greg and I began hanging out in a disguised plutonic capacity until one evening Dr. Greg invited me over to watch a movie. I agreed to come over after I worked out and showered. I am proud that we made it through the movie, but the sexual tension had become so immense that I jumped him. Once the credits began to roll, I came across the couch like a lioness upon prey! Locking lips with Dr. Greg, the affair had begun. I enjoyed spending time with him because he was established, stable, sane, intelligent, and gorgeous, and furthermore, had an endearing way of making me feel the same. Dr. Greg and I spent almost every night for the next three months together, and I fell in love with him. I held back, but fighting my feelings only seemed to intensify them. Dr. Greg's sweet birthday gifts, home-made breakfasts, conversations, and confession of love for me were too much to emotionally resist. When he left to go to Lexington, he took a piece of my heart with him; missing this piece of my heart, I became insatiable. I began to acquire more and more sexual partners and eventually lost count. Dr. Greg had exited my life, and with him, so had my desire to love. It hurt. I never let him know just how much but with a broken heart as a testament of lost love, I was determined never to feel this destitute again.

My expendable use of men is not something I am proud of developing. I am proud that I no longer view men this way. I did not value myself during the promiscuous years I spent in Terminus. I did not see the point in allowing a man to hurt me again, so I engaged in one night stands and short lived courtships. I thought it was fabulous and somewhat of a game. Jack was always down for going out and performing so I did as well. What is interesting about these frivolous times is that I never went a day without prayer or meditation. My soul was despicably lost, and I felt wretched and ashamed. I enjoyed going out and being beautiful and admired, and the attention from men was superfluously stimulating, but the deep remorse and regret that ate away at my intestines the morning after never ceased from reoccurring. I was causing irrevocable damage to myself, and I did not even realize it was happening. The primary sources of pain that I consistently felt were coming down off of psychotropic drugs with nowhere to go but an empty bed (which at times was occupied by someone who cared for me as much as I cared for them), being openly gay and living a lifestyle that my parents were completely ignorant to, despising my job, and feeling myself become further and further from God. The lifestyle I was leading probably would have purchased me a one way ticket to hell, not for the act of sex, but for the incessant drug use, meaningless sex, vanity, and hedonism. I had become a monster, a gay, performing monster. My friends enjoyed me because I was the raw, comic relief and the one they could vicariously live their sex lives through. Fabulous. Gorgeous. Wonderful. This life was not what I wanted, but the fruits of acceptance and freedom were. I knew I needed to find a balance, but I did not know how. Jack did not seem to want to slow down, so we continued to perform. Weekend after weekend was filled with Blues, Frontstreet, Drake's, The Hairy Dick, circuit parties, after parties, sex, drugs, and debauchery.

I had become an addict. No particular drug, just the rush of being mentally altered. There was something so deeply disturbing and uncomfortable about just being me that I enjoyed being something else. I thought I was everything when I was high: gorgeous, desirable, witty, loved, high. The drug abuse that was currently occurring in my life made my high school use seem recreational. I often went into work at Enterprise without any sleep and twitching from withdrawals. These were tricky, turbulent times, and I showed no sign of slowing down.

Sleep Consciousness and a Wake Up Call

My cousin, Ollie, graduated from high school in June of 2004, and I flew home to celebrate this tremendous milestone with him and my family. It was great being home over a period of time unaffiliated with a holiday. I had forgotten how beautiful spring in Virginia was and how much I missed my family and friends. The night before my departure from Virginia back to Georgia, I decided to go out and test drive my Terminus tactics on the small time gays of Hampton Roads. I went to a Norfolk night club, The Wave, and caught the eye of a blonde surfer type guy. He was perspiring with masculinity and putty in my hands. The drinks continued to flow up until last call, and then, similar to the Terminus scene, we made way to Bugottis, the afterhours spot. By the time we left Bugottis, I was barely able to stand. The surfer gentleman said he lived close by and that I was welcome to follow him home and crash. This invitation was what I had been anticipating all night, so I accepted and drove steadily behind him towards his home.

In the condition that I was in, it was entirely through the grace of God that I arrived at his townhouse alive and without a DUI. I made a decision to have intercourse with him and after the deed had been done, I promptly passed out into a drunken sleep. I was in a place somewhere between sleep and consciousness and having eerie difficulty trying to figure out if what was happening to me was reality or a dream. I was strangely unable to tell what was actually going on, like those dreams that are so surreal that you seldom realize you are dreaming until some harsh element of reality, such as the red lights of your alarm clock or the familiar scent of your dog places you in reality. But somehow, I knew that there was a foreign object inside of me. As I lay in this stranger's bed on my stomach, the blurred thoughts of what was happening were surfacing in my mind. I did have intercourse with him, but I did not remember consenting to a second occurrence, but was I dreaming? I reached my hand around in order to be able to have a tangible medium to what could have been a dream, and I felt a condomless penis penetrating me. Instantly, I catapulted into complete consciousness. I struggled to get this violator off of me and in a fit of rage began to strike him in the chest. I could not believe what was happening and how another person could take the liberty of another's body. I was disgusted with him and moreover disgusted with myself. After collecting my garments and self, I made a tumultuous trip back to my parents' home.

The next morning, the celebration of Ollie's graduation continued at a breakfast buffet at Golden Corral. I was out of my body in disbelief, agony, and anguish. I felt as if I would never eat another morsel of food again. Forcing smiles and laughter, my family recognized that there was something wrong, but I told them that I had a rough evening and just needed to rest. After breakfast, my parents drove me to the airport and as always, we hugged goodbye, but I did not feel as if this were a typical valediction. It was invariably ominous; as I hugged my mother, I felt her arousing vibrancy. As I hugged my father, I felt his stern and estranged love. This farewell was like a final emancipation and delivery unto the electric chair. I had been raped.

Upon arriving back in Terminus, I went into social reclusion, temporarily refusing to speak to my friends when they called and abandoning my old habits of sexual exploitation and drug abuse. I emerged from the lachrymose walls of my apartment solely to go to work and suffered in silence the mental grief of being utterly violated and possibly contracting an incurable disease. During the three months that I waited having to go and get tested for a STD contraction, my mind went down a path of shame and regret. I pondered thoughts that this unfortunate experience was somehow my fault. I felt that because I made a life of meaningless sexual encounters, I had gotten what I deserved. Food lost its taste, music became mute, and for the first time in my life I felt chronically depressed. Whatever sound trace of my relationship with God that had been cultivated so many years ago that was present told me to turn to Him. I prayed and read *The Bible* religiously. Were my behaviors truly the cause for what happened to me? Had God abandoned me? I specifically remember thinking that Jesus thought God had forsaken him as well. According to Romans 5:8, God demonstrates His love for us in this, "While we were still sinners, Christ died for us." I know that the front of what I was feeling is not comparable to what Jesus endured or the feelings of alienation and abandonment he must have felt, but how beautiful is it that Jesus, who loves us enough to bear the cross, has felt more pain than we can imagine? Jesus understands what we experience because he suffered a much greater pain. I had not been deserted. I had been found. I had received a merciful wakeup call.

On the day of my test results, I opened my Bible one last time for my final benediction before discovering my fate. My fingers casually turned to a page on which my eyes casually glanced at the words: *God keeps his promises.* My body began to tingle from my fingers and my toes inward toward my chest and heart. I felt the most ultimate high, beyond any drug I had ever ingested, surge through my limbs with a force I can only describe as purity. I was filled with the Holy Spirit. When I got to the medical center, it was as if I was not walking alone, but amongst angels. The elevator had become a chariot to victory; the medical corridors were a road to God's forgiveness for my self-serving behaviors. And inside the office and on my results paper appeared *Negative;* Praise Him, through the grace of God, I was negative! I had experienced my first miracle. I had awakened from the interim of sleep and consciousness.

Black Sparrow

How might one who has recently experienced God's everlasting grace be expected to behave? Grateful, for my fate could have been disastrous. Repented, my previous behaviors had led me to a den of inequity. Passionate, experiencing Christ's forgiveness is great enough to wake up any sleeping sinner... but for how long? I tried to lead a reformed lifestyle, God knows I tried, but it was too difficult for my weak spirit and my dwindling gratitude, repentance-conviction, and passion. It was no longer than a month before I was back in the clubs again and in the bed of a stranger. God still continued to bless me. I was hired as a field marketing manager with the largest alcohol distribution company in the world, Diageo. So I said, "Farewell," to Enterprise and, "pleased to meet you," to quarterly stipends to drink, unlimited access to clubs and parties, samples and a license to transport them in my company car, and down... down... down... down. Instead of taking advantage of this new opportunity, I let the opportunity take advantage of me. The next three years working at Diageo were turbulent: I bought my first piece of real estate, a two bedroom condo downtown, I jumped a tax bracket in salary, I traveled more than I ever had, I became disillusioned with how superficially fabulous my life seemed. Throughout this time, my life can be summarized as a ritual. I dated men but never longer than a few weeks. It was as if once I had been with them sexually, all of the luster and newness immediately evaporated into thin air. I attribute this to the still hostile existence of my need to feel validated and desired. Once I realized this, regardless of the lustful nature of the occurrence and subsequent superficial validation, I emotionally moved on. I was scared. I did not possess enough substance to sustain a healthy relationship with anyone and I knew it. My use of drugs went from recreational to habitual, years of redundant behaviors yielded the ultimate truth that I had become an oversexed drug addict. Deep in my heart, I knew I wanted to quit this life of faux fabulous hardships, but my convictions were too weak and my self-worth weaker. I could not do it on my own. I prayed, cried, and went in to get tested when things became scary. All the time, I thanked Jesus for sparing me, but I was never able to change my mentality or behaviors. Looking back at this period of my life, it is one that many gays fall victim to. I believe the escape that drugs provided allowed me to feel secure in whom I was and caused me to ignore what I had become. The temporary love or insatiable lust I stock-posted was false proof that I was desirable and that somebody saw the value in me. Most of the people I misconceived as friends were undoubtedly accomplices as they accompanied me in the horrific escape car of self-destruction. Two weeks after I decided that I needed to change my life, I met someone who did just that.

This Chapter might have had a completely different tone before yesterday. However, today I was reminded of the beauty of forgiveness. I spent almost four years of my life in an emotionally abusive relationship, and transcendently

I can now experience freedom from the negative emotions that I harbored. In my life, I have prayed hard for forgiveness. God has forgiven me, therefore I should forgive others. My natural instinct is to seek revenge, but I have found that taking advantage of the opportunity that God has given me to forgive is so much more effective. Resentment does not work for two reasons: The person you are resenting more than likely does not care and it will manifest into something much worse than it started out. Resentment lives in a bitter heart, and those who are bitter do not seek forgiveness because they are too caught up in hate. I will need forgiveness in the future, so I must learn to forgive in the present.

I suppose the four years of this relationship was like playing house, or Duck,Duck Goose. I never truly loved my ex. I believe that the illusion of what he could potentially offer was too overwhelmingly positive to deny. He was stable, drug-free, supposedly Christian, seemingly honest, and even more so seemingly sane. I was unstable, addicted, fallen, weak, and demoralized. I was ready to pursue happiness. As a child who chooses a *goose* they envisage a challenge in chasing them until they are securely seated back in the circle of safety, I selected a partner I felt would pursue me on my quest to wellbeing. I never thought that he would cheat on me, attack me, lie to me, manipulate me, control me, or provoke me. I definitely was not innocent in the relationship, there are always two parties involved, the difference is that I was always willing to accept my responsibility and the other party was not. It is baffling to realize that four years of my life were spent being tortured, miserable, and unfulfilled. This pain seems insignificant because God has given me the power to forgive my ex, and I have entirely moved on.

Now I can focus on the good that the relationship brought into my life. I left Diageo and became a Literature teacher, something that is not only rewarding but that I love and am gifted at doing. Jack and I were temporarily forced to go our separate ways, which gave us both sobriety and stability, eventually resulting in Jack relocating to another state to fulfill his amazing potential. I also have learned what I need from a relationship and how not to sacrifice who I am, my friends, or my family in the process of obtaining it. And finally, I have freed my heart to love in a healthy, trusting, infidelity free relationship with a partner who is capable of accepting his responsibility in conflict while also forgiving me for my mistakes. Holistically, instead of heading down… down… down… down… these four years of my life have positioned and prepared me to look up.

The answer to the question *can I love myself* depends on how an individual sees his or herself. Unfortunately, the way I see myself is a product of many external ideals and influences, some positive and some negative. I have been so focused on the negative that I have neglected logic and my God given wisdom. I do not know why my younger self dwelled on the ignorant belief that God does not like gays or that a gay lifestyle connotes damnation and hell. The wasteful nature of trying to correct something about myself that was natural to me caused me to overlook those things that were unnatural. I ignored the self-indulgence, dishonesty, hate, jealousy, sexual objectification, reprisal, greed, self-destruction, and idolization--all changeable afflictions--to hone in on my homosexuality, which I have about as much chance in changing as I do in altering the color of my eyes.

Jesus does not see me the way that I see myself or in the manner other Christians or the world view me. Therefore, it is counterproductive to judge myself or take any criticism and hate spewed my way to heart. I am a black sparrow and here I stand to soar. I find it to be wonderful because I am firmly planted with both feet on the ground. From here I can see what I was never able to see before; that I have wings and that I *can* fly. Sparrows do not automatically enter into a successful first flight-- they fall, waiver, and teeter before finally gracing the skies. The next attempt a sparrow makes to leave the ground, it has learned from failed experiences and found an internal balance and streamlined equilibrium. So, how can anyone judge what is free in flight on the wings of their personal experiences *and* in the arms of the Lord? I shall constantly persevere and strive to be my personal best. Jesus knows the character of my heart and that character is beautiful yet undeniably flawed. The opportunity to renew myself in his love and mercy is all that I need and can ever ask for. I am grateful that Jesus loves me regardless of what anyone has said and will ever say about me.